# The

# MAN

# CODE

WHITNEY L. WOODS, PH.D.

The Man Code

© 2020 by Whitney L. Woods

U.S. Copyright Office File#1-9842142082

ISBN: 978-1-09835-392-6

ISBN eBook: 978-1-09835-393-3

All Rights Reserved

*Hierogrammat Publications*

*wwoods1@mi.rr.com*

*Oakland County, Michigan*

*Printed in the United States of America*

# CONTENTS

# UNIT THREE
## *Resources*

# UNIT FOUR
## *Calling*

## UNIT FIVE

## *Self-Defense*

### Chapter Five: Security: To Be Forewarned Is To Be Forearmed

# THE MAN CODE (TMC): AN INTRODUCTION

This work is the culmination of more than a half century of observations and personal and collective vicarious and direct experience and research. The theories presented here are the response to a growing chorus of voices stating, "You should write a book." Over time, I became more and more assertive in vocalizing these ideas, which meant that there were moments when the dialogues became very heated. I was pushing the envelope to ensure its contents were valid.

I was also gauging the reactions of friends, foes, colleagues and the like to hone and refine this information. I openly sought evidence to the contrary because I was shocked at how frequent my theses went unchallenged. Though pleased that there was a high level of agreement with the Man Theories, my academic training, as well as common sense, taught me that uncovering the truth also meant the search for confounding evidence.

So where was this data collected? Where wasn't it would probably be an easier answer. The list of venues used for this book include schools at all levels, company break rooms and board rooms, bars and barbershops, gyms, arenas, athletic fields, stadiums, basements, locker rooms, restaurants, doctors' offices, churches, lunchrooms, automobile plants, stairwells, parking lots and street corners.

I've also literally incorporated the perspectives of those from one to 100 and across all cultural landscapes and educational levels. I believe Verse One from the *The Instructions of Ptahhotep: The Oldest Book in the World* is instructive: "Do not be proud and arrogant with your knowledge. Consult and converse with the ignorant and the wise, for the limits of art are not reached...Good speech is more hidden than greenstone (emeralds), yet it may be found among the maids at the grindstones."

In other words, wisdom is not the sole property of the well educated and well heeled: it can be found anywhere! That said, despite the diverse points of view presented, it is for the reader to decide how he will interpret and use these theories. I do not claim that all will be receptive and that the ideas will apply to ALL men in ALL circumstances. To the contrary, the READER MUST discuss and debate, internally and otherwise, this information and its responsible application.

The examples and case studies provided are merely instruments for your toolbox. For some, that means adding utensils, for others, it means you are already well equipped. For all, including myself, this essay is an opportunity to reflect on what is manhood and how do we define it? A female colleague once told me, "A man says what he means, and means what he says." This is an old adage and our essay allows us to address its validity as well as that of similar statements.

Finally, just because I have given an idea the status of Man Code, does not preclude it from being a trait or attribute admirable for a woman. In this day and age, where we increasingly find women as head of households and raising children on their own, role definitions are constantly being challenged. However, when and where men ARE present, whether inside or outside of the home, we will not stop holding ourselves to certain ideals! We would never suggest, for instance, that it is wrong for a man to have a role in the maintenance of a home. But that does not mean neglecting responsibilities in the arenas of protection and provisions.

The following selected Man topics are submitted for your inspection and approval (or disapproval). I do not claim that they are all encompassing. Furthermore, one can reject the Codes at their own peril. But, as an artist in our popular culture stated, "That don't STOP REALITY from BEING REAL!" Enjoy!!

# CHAPTER ONE:

# *Bullying: Addressing The Elephant In The Room*

**This chapter will discuss** common conflicts inevitable in one's evolution from a youth to grown man status. As in all chapters, I've dropped in some personal examples. The purpose of the stories is to provoke thought and reflection. It should be easy to make analogies and comparisons to your own experience, especially for an adult reader—that is the intention. It's very possible that you may recall a situation even more prominent and dramatic than the ones provided. This is also good because the goal is to have a running dialogue as you move through the text.

The point is not to glamorize violence as a means to resolve conflicts. In fact, if we do nothing else, we should promote its avoidance, and where possible, ask did WHATEVER CHOICE WE MADE ACHIEVE THE DESIRED OUTCOME? After stating a Man Code, an object study will be given. As we close, we will review lessons learned and ponder how this data may inform future actions.

Currently, bullying is a hot topic. It appears you can't view news or contemporary events without someone claiming they are a victim. However, we as keepers and practitioners of the Man Code don't get it. From my perspective, the children of the 1960's and 1970's, not to mention earlier eras, never seriously considered whether we were being "bullied." Why? Because many of us weren't running in the house complaining about another child whupping our butts, and those who did, were told to go back out, and, in some instances, not to come back until we settled it ourselves. If the adversary were a child that were much older or an adult, now that's a different story!

You fought your own battles and win or lose, you generally lived to tell another tale. This taught young men the independence and aggression necessary to survive. Weapons were generally frowned upon as an act of cowardice and only considered if one were outnumbered or at a gross disadvantage. In addition, if you picked a fight with a child who had physical or mental challenges, you lost all respect and suffered endless ridicule.

There are two more rules I can add to the above. First, a conflict, whether it arose on the basketball court, the schoolhouse, or in your neighborhood, was generally between TWO individuals. You could be fighting a classmate and his brother and a friend could be standing right there. They were only present to stop the fracas if it got out of hand, or provide "assistance" or as a deterrent to others thinking of joining the fray. The onlookers might give pugilistic commentary or simply say, "that's enough" and pull you off each other. They would not jump in because it was not **THEIR FIGHT.**

If your hands were good that day, your opponent might ask their entourage, "Why didn't you help?" If their response were on code, they would say, **"BECAUSE IT WAS ONE ON ONE!"**

A second standard was that yesterday's opponent could be today's ally. If the two of you were allowed to engage each other, whether in sport or fisticuffs, you gained the other's respect. The next go round, that same young man may see you having a problem and offer his help.

There are those of you who may believe what I am describing is a young male utopia. This is partly because of the uneven rules of engagement YOU may have witnessed. The Man Code SHOULD be an inter-generational conversation anyway. Merely a few decades ago, it was uncommon for young men to be in the house all day playing violent video games instead of outdoors playing until the sun set. Should we be surprised that the first time someone lays a hand on these fingernail gangsters, they're ready to blast?

## MAN CODE 1:1: IF PEOPLE CAN TAKE ADVANTAGE OF YOU, THEY WILL

I heard dad say this once. When I was about five years old, I began to understand why. Our family lived in a then Co-Op known as Parkway Gardens on the Southside of Chicago, Illinois. At that time, in the early 1960's, unbeknownst to us, Michelle Robinson, who would grow up to be First Lady Michelle Obama, lived there too. Now, Parkway Gardens is one of the most notorious housing projects in America. One day, I had two dollars and was given permission to go buy some candy at the drug store on the corner of 63rd and South Parkway Avenue (near the L Train Station) with my cousin Fred, who was the same age.

Mission accomplished! As I crossed South Parkway while returning with my bag of goodies, I had a genius idea. I was determined to take two to three minutes off of what was only a 15-minute trip. "Fred, let's take a short cut." Instead of walking south on South Parkway, the main street, we could cut through the alley/playground of the elementary school on the corner and enter our building from the back. As we got halfway through this truncated route, we were approached by two older boys who looked to be at least 16. "Let me have the bag," one of them said while simultaneously reaching for it. "What you got in your pockets?" was next as he ran his hands through them, pulling out the loose change I had left. They did the same to Fred, but to no avail, Fred didn't have any money.

Only later did it occur to me why I was crying and Fred wasn't when we returned to my grandmother's. In fact, my cousin had a quizzical look on his face as if he were wondering, 'What's wrong with him?' He couldn't feel my pain because he didn't lose anything! At the moment, I felt the loss of innocence and a small amount of candy. Were my cousin and I "bullied?" Probably not, certainly when you consider the times. It was just business as usual on the Southside.

But looking back on it, Fred and I were lucky we were not physically harmed. I also learned a valuable lesson. Even prior to this incident, the elders always warned us never to take short cuts. Now, I had an object lesson why. To this day, I rarely take the alley.

Anytime a young man can learn a lifesaving lesson and come out relatively unscathed, should be cause for celebration. Those who insulate our youth from age-appropriate adversity, are doing them a disservice.

## MAN CODE 1:2 THERE IS ALWAYS SOMEONE BIGGER AND BADDER THAN YOU

As a high school teacher, I related a lot of my lessons to mental and physical toughness. Sometimes, the young men would brag, "Mr.

Woods, I never lost a fight," in their quest to impress me and their classmates. It didn't work. My retort, "It's probably because you never fought anybody."

Muhammad Ali was the "Greatest" because he fought in an era of great heavyweights. He lost and regained his title three times. He was the champion of champions, beating Joe Frazier, George Foreman, Leon Spinks, and Ken Norton. No other fighter before or since can lay claim to such a portfolio. In a similar manner, we must encourage our youth not to shy away from competition since it is what defines their greatness.

I was fortunate enough to be in the presence of youth who excelled inside and outside of the classroom. One such young man was point guard Michael Talley, Michigan's Mr. Basketball in 1989. The Detroit Cooley High School team he captained, was the last in Michigan to win three consecutive state championships in Class A, the largest division.

I was one of Mike's teachers as a substitute at Cerveny Middle School. I used to play basketball with him and his center Daniel Lyton, after school in Cerveny's gym in the school's basement. When Mike got to high school, I would run pickup basketball games with him and Danny, who was also all-state, on Saturdays at a local community college. But Mike wasn't playing against other kids, he was playing with and against grown men such as myself.

Now fast forward 25 more years, and Mike is the basketball coach and Dean of Students at a high school where I was teaching. I reminded him that I was one of his teachers in middle school as well as a teammate in those pickup games where you had to win because it might have been hours before you got back on the court. Mike told me that back then, he was always looking for top-notch competition, so he borrowed his mother's car to ride out there on those Saturday nights.

Mike filled me in on some details I didn't know about his background. He was from Brightmoor, a rough neighborhood on Detroit's Westside. "When I looked out my door, on the left were the dope dealers, gang members, and drug addicts. On the right, was the playground. That's the direction I headed in." Talley's journey led him to the University of Michigan. There, he was instrumental in recruiting fellow Detroiters Jalen Rose and Chris Webber, as well as the other three members of what would later be known as The Fab Five. This recruitment was the ultimate sacrifice, because while it meant the team was better, Mike's playing time was reduced.

Mike Talley would also win a state championship as a coach with a team starring his son, Mike Talley Jr. Coach Talley told me he set the example by demanding that Michael Jr. follow in his footsteps, not just on the court, but in the classroom. "When his grades would dip, we would put the gloves on and go in the basement."

However, some of my students weren't impressed. As the school's dean, Mike was compassionate but firm. I loved his approach, because he supported the teaching staff 100%. "This man is teaching you lessons beyond the classroom" he kept telling the boys, some whom he coached. But there were those who resented Mike's "bend but don't break" disciplinary philosophy, and knowing he was an all-time favorite former student of mine, decided to impugn his character.

"He (Coach Talley) was garbage at Michigan," one of my male students said for the whole class' listening pleasure. His peers knew this young man's comment was meant as a challenge. I shut the lesson down right then and there. You could hear a pin drop!

This moment was akin to the needle being abruptly pulled off the record at a party. "Can you name one thing that you are the best at in the state of Michigan?" I asked. "Tiddlywinks? Tonk? **ANYTHING! BECAUSE, SON, IN 1989, COACH TALLEY WAS THE BEST BASKETBALL PLAYER IN THE STATE!!!**"

In the hysteria over the "bullying crisis," we as adult men must ensure that while safeguarding our youth from unnecessary harm, that we don't wrap them in a plastic bubble which prevents them from becoming men. Conflicts and clashes, within limits, are what defines our youth, and will assist them in gaining the confidence and toughness necessary for future success. A common theme in the conversations I've had with the men who have framed this study, is that we **all** have a day of reckoning—when we cannot avoid those who stand in our path.

We tend to think of a "bully" as someone who is in our way. But what about the "bully" within? At some point, we have to confront our internal fears, demons, and phobias. Although bullies may be viewed with a mix of awe and amazement, in reality, by nature, they are highly insecure. What else would explain why grown men would rob or terrorize old women or little kids? In all likelihood, they are just doing what was done to them. A real man realizes that just because he **CAN** do something, doesn't mean he **SHOULD**. There's something called karma and while boys have excuses, men have responsibilities.

As mentioned above, what ever happened to the ethics of engagement? We've seem to lost our way with adults jumping into kids' scraps, many-on-one massacres (that's not a "fight"), and the belief that virtual interaction (computer or video) is the same as a hard-fought game of pickup basketball.

Lest we not forget, there is a day of reckoning for the bully too. At one Eastside high school where I taught, there was a 6'5" 370 pound kid who was nicknamed "Bus Stop." When I learned that he earned this moniker by knocking out a **GIRL** at a bus stop near a school he was kicked out of, I lost all respect for him. While others, including the school's staff, called him by his nickname, I stuck with the name his mother gave him. At this point in my career, I was an administrator, so part of my job was discipline.

On days when I would be clearing the hall, I'd sometimes catch "Bus Stop" leaning on a wall reluctant to budge. After imploring him to go to class, I would sometimes be met with, "F--- YOU, I'M NOT GOING ANYWHERE, LEAVE ME THE F--- ALONE!!" Since "Bus Stop" was a football player, I would get on the walkie talkie and ask the Athletic Director, also an Assistant Principal, to take my write up and deal with it. The AD would talk to "Bus Stop" and send him to class as if nothing happened.

One morning, as students walked in through the school's metal detector, "Bus Stop" got into a verbal altercation with a kid who was new to the school. The AD asked me to take the boys into an office near the front door and sit with these young men until he could talk to them. I did as instructed. In the office, "Bus Stop" continued to run his mouth, trying to intimidate the new kid on the block. The other young man, while not as big as "Bus Stop," was not little either. He was about 6' 3" 190 pounds. His response to "Bus Stop's" "bullying" certainly got my attention. "Oh **yeah?**" the young man said calmly. "We'll **SEE** when we get **outside.**"

By his even-keeled retort to "Bus Stop's" attempts at intimidation, I deduced several things about this young man: 1) He wasn't scared 2) He probably wasn't planning on acting alone 3) He might have intended on using some heat 4) This kid **REALLY** was from the streets and, 5) All of the above. In any event, the new kid was taken seriously, because a few weeks later, "Bus Stop" was run off his own campus. Because of the threats he received, "Bus Stop" was sent home permanently along with his schoolwork. Not surprisingly, years later, one of his former classmates informed me that "Bus Stop" was in jail.

Remember, the Code is that there's always someone bigger and badder than you and everyone wants to be a gangster until the **REAL** ones arrive on the set. Perhaps, our young men could benefit by taking a page from Kevin's book. Kevin, who is in his 40's, gives boxing lessons and trains at a gym in metropolitan Detroit. The other day, I peeked into a studio at this facility and saw him putting in some work on the heavy bag.

I entered and began verbally sparring with him. "Come on, man," I kidded, "as big as you are, ain't nobody going to mess with you." "I don't know," Kevin replied. "There's some crazy ones out there." I decided to return fire. "Well, as Mike Tyson said, 'everybody's got a plan until they get hit in the mouth.'" "I don't **PLAN** on getting hit in the mouth," he countered.

# CHAPTER 2:

## *What's Love Got To Do With It?*

**In our last chapter,** we discussed the undeniable reality that when there is discord, particularly among young men, that conflict, and sometimes violence, are inevitable. No one is immune. Also, no one is **INVINCIBLE.** If you don't believe every dog has his day, you haven't lived long enough. Manning up means taking your lumps and using the lessons learned to move forward. The good news is that sports and even strenuous physical and manual labor are acceptable, and sometimes even profitable outlets, for redirecting such energy.

In this chapter, we will examine topics that can't be adequately addressed through sole reliance on one's physical prowess. In fact, purely emotional and physical reactions to the issues posed will be exposed as weakness. Instead, we will have to use a little more of that space between our ears. Why? Because this time, the scenarios are not intramural—they deal with appropriate responses to dilemmas inherent in our interaction with women.

There comes a time in a young man's life when he becomes interested in, as they say in the South, 'them gals.' Ideally, however, a boy's first priority should be maturing and developing the discipline and skills necessary for him to be a protector and provider if he is to ever to be considered a man. Otherwise, he'll be a rudderless ship and any relationship he has with the opposite sex will render him lost and turned out.

We now have an excellent opportunity to debunk a common fallacy: the sooner a young man experiences a young lady, the sooner he grows up. At this point, a conscious and mature adult male needs to step in and have **the talk** with him. But not all men are built to lead this conversation. Unfortunately, some men seem hell-bent on the next generation repeating the same mistakes that made them who they are: ignorant, irresponsible and immature! Let's see what the Code says about young boys engaging young girls in such a manner.

## MAN CODE 2:1 HAVING SEX DOESN'T MAKE YOU A MAN, BEING ABLE TO HANDLE THE CONSEQUENCES OF HAVING SEX DOES

So many of our young men are lost on this point, especially if their guidance is coming from their peers, that it's like the blind leading the blind. Let's take Alton, for example. He was a single child whose dad had a good job in the plant and bought Alton every game and toy on the planet. By seventh grade, Alton was popular and athletic—he also wanted you to know he was having sex. In case you had a bad memory, he reminded you of this everyday.

But Alton wasn't selfish. He would invite his friends to go with him, in the event you wanted to join in. "She doesn't care." Of course, the braggadocio surrounding his antics only intensified when Alton got to high school. After graduation, he signed up for the military. Alton wanted to make the most of his time before he reported, and we all know what that meant. As fate would have it, Alton got into an argument with one of his girlfriends. Alton was so busy bragging about his sexual exploits with these girls, he forgot to include one key detail—he was also beating them! But this one retaliated. She stabbed Alton to death with a butcher knife. The young lady was never charged because she was considered to be acting in self-defense!

## MAN CODE 2:2 YOU CAN NEVER WIN AN ARGUMENT WITH A WOMAN

Granddad used to say, "I always keep my hat near the door." It took me a few years to understand this comment. He and my grandmother on my mother's side seemed perfect for each other. She was fire and he was ice. They were resilient people; it's just that she was more talkative, and granddad was that alpha male who was the strong and silent type. Though equally yoked, there were times they were not on the same page. Generally, grandmother would be the one to voice her disapproval. Granddad would make his point and disengage. If she continued, he would say, "Okay sugah, Okay sugah," as if he were repeating a magic chant. When this didn't work, granddad would get up from his favorite chair and start walking toward the back door. He would grab his hat on the way out and jump in his Oldsmobile. The car would start and he would take off.

Granddad would be gone for 30 minutes to an hour. When he returned, it was all quiet on the home front. More often than not, grandmother would be sitting quietly on the living room couch knitting and watching television. Crisis aborted!

## MAN CODE 2:3 WOMEN FIGHT WITH THEIR MOUTHS, AND MEN FIGHT WITH THEIR HANDS

This gem comes from Yosha, a former police officer in Flint, Michigan, a community with one of the highest violent crime rates per capita, according to the Federal Bureau of Investigations. She is also a mother of four, including two adult males who are in law enforcement themselves. "The worst calls were for domestic violence," Yosha said. "Most of the time, a man and a woman would get into an argument and the woman wouldn't stop talking. The man would just snap."

The days when responding officers could be reassured by a couple that everything is fine and leave, are a relic of the past. On too many occasions, the officers would depart, only to discover later, that the quarrel was reinvigorated and a physical assault occurred. Thus, laws were changed and most police departments that make a domestic violence run, have to take someone with them. Obviously, men can be victims too, and attacks against men are on the rise. But for now, let's entertain the prospect that the assailant is a man.

The perception of male assailants is based on the fact that men are generally stronger. Law enforcement and criminal justice systems take all of this into account in the charging, prosecution, and sentencing of male offenders. Therefore, the Man Code requires that men be highly disciplined in all interactions with their female counterparts, from the recruitment and dating phases to sexual intercourse and ultimately, living together. Of course, this is easier said than done, particularly when children are present.

Avoidance of a physical altercation is always the best policy. Some men are able to do this simply by going into or even sleeping in "the other room." One award-winning basketball coach said sometimes he just goes in the bathroom and locks the door. Still others are able to accomplish this by the strategy discussed in 2:2, or by going for a walk or taking up a sport or "quiet time" activity to keep them constructively occupied or distracted. One gentleman, who is a welder, said he and his wife went to counseling. He claimed she stopped because the therapist wasn't always "siding with her." These sessions were helping **him**, so he continued attending on his own.

It goes without saying that each man must do what works for him. There is no one size fits all approach that could ever work for everybody. We also have to be honest enough to admit that after avoidance, diversions, counseling, seeking the wisdom of one's fellows, and even prayer, nothing may help. It may be time to throw in the towel. Those who are living in misery and are "staying together for the kids," need to think about what kind of example they are setting for them.

## MAN CODE 2:4 I'M GOING TO RESPECT YOU AND YOU ARE GOING TO RESPECT ME

We all know the consequences of a man losing his head when dealing with a female. One of the maxims society has embedded in us is "**never**" hit a woman. As a general rule, the Man Code supports this. However, that does not mean, under **any** circumstances, that we are waiving our right to defend ourselves. We should not be calling women out of their name. They should not be calling us out of ours either! As soon as the opportunity presents itself, a man should make abundantly clear that he will not tolerate verbal or physical assaults. "You're going to respect me and I am going to respect you." Then make sure that you practice what you preach! Do not accept her excuse that, "I was just mad," or "I was just emotional."

If such behavior becomes more frequent, especially early on, you might need to be looking at the front door. Men would have been born strapped to the ceiling if we were meant to be punching bags. A security officer once got into an argument with a woman he was dating. She took the liberty to start hitting him. Before Officer Johnson retaliated, he informed her, "You were a girl before, but you're a **WOMAN NOW!!**" Johnson then explained to her family what transpired. Needless to say, that was their last rodeo together. To stay in such a relationship would be what we call "graveyard love."

Remember, men can be victims too, and often, the process starts early. Edwin was one of the biggest and strongest kids in his neighborhood. As a tackle on his youth football team, Edwin's backs loved running behind him, because he could clear a hole big enough to drive an 18-wheeler through. The little girls, however, saw and exploited a weakness in this gentle giant. These young ladies would be frequently found wailing on him for no reason. "You could tell his mother told him to 'never hit a girl,'" a childhood teammate said. As a result, Edwin never gained the full respect of his male peers.

Women are beautiful, wondrous and complex creatures. Anytime a man can enjoy a positive relationship with a woman, especially one that is long-term, he is very fortunate. But in order for us to be that rock, we must educate ourselves about some common misconceptions. Some relate to our notions of concepts like fidelity.

## MAN CODE 2:5 THERE ARE THREE FORMS OF FIDELITY OR INFIDELITY: EMOTIONAL, FINANCIAL, AND PHYSICAL

We are going to steer clear of infantile terms such as cheating, which may be an example of a physical indiscretion. The reason I say may is that unless you are on the inside, you don't know what that couple's agreement is—they **may** be in an open relationship. Beyond that, unless two people plan on spending all their time in bed, there are other issues that must be considered. This is not to say that polygamy is okay. If that presents a problem for you, then tell your partner that you want to be physically exclusive with them. In this respect, there's only a problem if this tenet is violated. At that point, you have a decision to make.

Emotional fidelity is being there for your mate, so that they don't feel alone or neglected. This is important as well. Humans have an incredible ability to empathize, love, and understand each other. If you feel you aren't being attended to in this area, that should also be expressed. Some frame this as spending quality or adult time with one another, however the two of you define it.

A third form of fidelity, particularly for couples living together, is financial. For instance, if two incomes are required, your financial goals, practices and priorities need to peacefully co-exist in order to survive. You or your mate might not be sleeping with someone else, but you both may find yourselves sleeping somewhere else, if the mortgage is not paid! A friend told me he came home from a hard day's work and flipped the light switch. The room was not illuminated. He asked his wife what happened, and he found out she bought some shoes. From that point on, he was responsible for paying the bills. After 30 years, their lights are still on.

Now, let's look at the consequences of affairs, particularly with those whom you **know** are not in open relationships. Previously, we addressed that just because you **can** do something, doesn't mean you should. Discretion is the better part of valor, and wisdom separates boys from men. A key piece of advice for engaging women you know are **supposed** to be with another man: **DON'T!!!** The Man Code does not advise you to avoid them for moral reasons, as much as for your own safety.

How can we be protectors if we put ourselves in harm's way? I'd like to debunk one more myth: being with another man's woman is nothing to brag about, it actually showcases ignorance since you should have left such childish methods of keeping score behind in your youth (recall Alton). A man once knew his wife was having an affair with a prominent public figure. This left him feeling embarrassed. One day, his emotions got the best of him and he watched his wife get into the car with her lover, his wife's supervisor, who was also married, and followed them to a hotel.

They went into a room. The distraught husband got out of his car and was soon at their door. But several of this public figure's security team, who were armed, told him he could not go in. The spurned husband left. A homicide detective familiar with this incident, boasted that he wouldn't have been barred entry to a room with his wife and another man in it. When asked what he would have done, he responded, "We would have had to shoot it out!" Though we can all empathize with the emotions of one of our brethren who wasn't informed that he was in an open marriage, is "shooting it out" really the answer?

This man's wife was not forcibly taken to the hotel room. She wasn't even raped. His wife went of her own volition. We must ask ourselves what happens the next time our spouse chooses to sleep with someone else? The point is you can't go around shooting all your problems. The married public servant, who is currently incarcerated, can only blame himself for being in a predicament where he could have incurred the deadly wrath of another husband. The disgruntled husband ended up getting a divorce from his wife.

Our next husband caught his wife in the act and gave her paramour a unique option. A woman thought her husband was out of town, so she invited her lover over. There was only one problem--her "significant other" hadn't actually left. The woman's husband, who was in the military, entered the apartment and startled the two lovebirds, to say the least. Loverboy hastily threw on his clothes and tried to walk past the soldier as if to say, 'I'll let you two talk.' The husband made it clear, however, there was only one way Romeo was getting out. "You're not going through that door. The only way you're leaving here is out the window." Fortunately, the couple lived on the second floor!

## 2:6 IN THE FIGHT TOGETHER

A man was accompanied by his girlfriend as he drove through a downtown jam-packed with traffic from a summer festival on the riverfront. Suddenly, another man bolted out of the passenger seat of an automobile attempting to merge from an adjoining parking lot. He stood in front of the car with the couple in it with his hands outstretched, as if he were the police directing traffic. The gentleman acting like a traffic officer yelled, **"STOP!"** allowing the second automobile to get in front. This rude display startled the couple because they were almost t boned by the intersecting vehicle.

As a result, the first car's driver was unequivocal in loudly announcing his disdain with this lawless exhibit since such reckless behavior, along with that of the merging car's driver, nearly caused an accident. The would-be cop hollered a nasty comment in response, before hastily jumping back into his side of the vehicle. Two young ladies in the backseat brought the total occupants to four. They drove off.

The man then asked his girlfriend if she were okay? She said yes. Next, he asked what she would have done had the driver and his three companions jumped out of the car in front of them and attacked him? "WE WOULD HAVE **ALL** BEEN OUT THERE FIGHTING!!" she said calmly, and without hesitation.

Of course, had this hypothetical played out, it would have been unfortunate. However, the girlfriend's reply aptly describes the mindset of a true partner. This was *her* man and she had no intent on being an innocent bystander as someone she loves was being assaulted. There would be no recording the incident on her phone or posting to social media, as if she were some dispassionate observer who merely sought to "document the attack," while awaiting the arrival of "the authorities." If need be, this woman were more than willing to jump into the fray. The script **she** was reading from said nothing about her role being that of a damsel in distress!

The above metaphor is appropriate because when you are in a solid, successful relationship, each partner is obligated to bring whatever the "fight" requires. Even though security generally falls within the purview of the man column, under extenuating circumstances, a good woman will always back up her significant other. Just as there are three forms of fidelity: emotional, physical, and financial, these are also the big three with respect to the support of a helpmate.

In a true union, particularly if the couple intends on living together, getting married (2:7) and/or having children, role definition and execution of the assigned duties, will determine its viability. In another era, the 1950's, for example, it probably would have been much simpler. Like clockwork, the man would be responsible for providing the financial resources and the physical maintenance of the grounds and the outside of the home as well as the clan's safety.

The woman would be the predominant nurturer and be responsible for cooking and cleaning and raising the children.

But since World War II, when women began joining the work-force in mass and haven't looked back, the family configuration looks radically different. The failures of the institution of marriage and other factors, have created more single parent families, joint custody, blended families, and grandparents raising their grandchildren.

But whatever the arrangement, when a man finds himself engaged in a long-term relationship with a woman, particularly if they share a household, it is reasonable for both to be clear about what each **brings to the table.** In one instance, a couple was prepar-ing to get married. They agreed to attend a pre-marital counseling session facilitated by one of their church's ministers. The minister, a woman, used a chalkboard in the church's basement to have them to do an intriguing activity. She had columns with significant cate-gories such as finances, taking out the garbage, cooking, cleaning, landscaping, etc. There were two rows. One had the groom's name, possessive form, and "Parents" in it, and the other had the bride's name, possessive form, and "Parents."

The pair was fortunate to have both sets of parents alive and still together. This was useful because the minister asked them who in their parents' homes performed the duties listed? Because these two were educated professionals, they quickly comprehended why a church official had them do such an exercise: it was to anticipate the role each would play in their survival as a unit.

Roles are not set in stone, however. Age, changes in health and work status as well as the household's familial composition, among other factors, can make them fluid. Over time, each duo must decide the level of tweaking necessary for them to continue to thrive.

Ironically, perhaps the best litmus test of a couple's compatibility is being apart. Many years ago, a young man and woman who were on the verge of starting a family, were going through a tumultuous period and decided to separate. For both, the split was an opportunity to look inward. Now, many years later, they are able to reflect on this experience. "When you are alone, there is nobody there but you. So you are forced to focus on yourself," the wife said.

A teaming approach has been critical to their longevity. The bedroom is no exception. "Some days, you may not want to go to work, but you do!" she added. Likewise, "you may not feel like it (being intimate), but you perform **anyway**, because that's **your job!!**" Her husband smiled, while nodding in agreement.

"Look, '**everyday** is not going to be **Sunday**,'" he stated, quoting his grandmother. "There are times when they (your mate) are carrying you, and there are times when you are **carrying them!!**"


## MAN CODE 2:7 MARRIAGE IS A LEGAL UNION

How often does a man find himself having to respond to, "do you think the two of you will get married?" after dating a woman for a short period of time. This question is asked as if marriage is the logical, linear, progression of any "serious" form of commitment. What is worse is the query is oft times initiated by someone who is married themselves, as if they are somehow probing into the quality of the relationship.

For most, comprehending marriage is like nailing jello on the wall. Let's start with what it isn't. A marriage ceremony may be held in a church, and still not be a spiritual union. As a preacher once said, "there are many people who are married, but are not wedded."

A couple reciting their vows can promise fidelity, but putting your name on a license does not force you to practice it. Nor does it guarantee you are aware of the three forms of it previously discussed. Being married does not necessarily mean a couple lives, eats, or even sleeps together, and this status cannot make them do so either.

A couple who is married might not even "get along." People have a litany of motives for getting married, from family and societal pressure to the fear of having a child out of wedlock. Moreover, a man and woman may genuinely love each other and want to do "the right thing." Marriage is one of the most materialistic institutions on the face of the earth and should not be entered into lightly. A wife once stated that during her ceremony, she said her vows before God. This may be true, but God doesn't determine if you're married or can get a divorce, THE COUNTY CLERK'S OFFICE DOES!

Therefore, any man thinking of getting hitched needs to spend just as much time talking to a lawyer as he does speaking to his fiancee's father. Why? Because of the legal and financial ramifications of this type of decision. Most of what people ascribe to marriage, is merely a discussion of two people who may live together. Grown folks spend so much time worrying about such immature topics as whether their prospective spouse is "cheating" (physical infidelity) on them, they forget to talk about serious survival issues like household finance (financial fidelity). While children may spend time checking each other's phones, adults need to check each other's bank accounts!

What makes marriage "serious" is not some mystical quality suddenly bestowed on a pair of lovers, but child naming rights, tax filing status, and the implications of divorce and estate planning, particularly in the event of the death of a spouse or family member.

Once more, men need counsel with attorneys and financial planners prior to our sit-down with a cleric!

Finally, some of us brag to our friends about how our union is going to be, or what we would and wouldn't put up with in a long-term relationship, particularly a marriage. Why not do some research? Find a husband and wife you admire who has been together 30, 40, or 50 or more years. Ask them what their journey was like before you make assumptions. As you look at what they have built, you might be surprised at how humbly they started out, and the obstacles they encountered along the way. It's easy for a young couple to get caught up in the pomp and circumstance of the proceedings. But in the long run, the couples who are winning, invested in **each other** and not just the ceremony!

# CHAPTER 3:

# *Modeling, Mentoring, And Male Bonding*

**Our last discussion centered** on dilemmas we face in dealing with our women, and strategies for how they might be handled. We suggested that a young man should not be pushed through the door of co-ed relations--he should enter when ready. Unfortunately, the notion that everyone is "doing it" is the result of negative peer pressure and the social and mass media's preoccupation with fulfilling flesh pleasures as a barometer of whether one has "come of age." Perhaps if we were born dogs, they would be correct.

It seems children are convinced that if they're not having sex by the age of 15 or 16, their genitals will fall off. In reality, a boy's singular focus should be his interpersonal development and accruing the habits of mind necessary to one day be considered a man. Furthermore, let us add that there is nothing wrong with engaging in adult behavior when one is actually an adult! We also tried to demystify fidelity and the true meaning of matrimony. In "Modeling,

Mentoring, and Male Bonding," the examination is in-house. We will explore where men can seek such guidance. We will look at concepts such as leadership, modeling and mentoring, and analyze how they are determined. Moreover, the discussion will be expanded as it will be argued that the Man Code identifies coaching and our receptivity to guidance, as an ongoing and critical lifelong process of adult male evolution.

Assuming that he is alive, one's father can be an optimal source for the values and dispositions necessary for male development. However, some fathers can be sub-optimal providers of this information for a variety of reasons. A first consideration is availability. Even when in the home, child-rearing may not be a priority. For others, the pull of career and various obligations may detract from them filling this role. But somehow, an exemplary parent always finds a way. "Being a parent is a full-time job," stated a father of five boys. "Even when I am at work, I have to be on call in case something happens."

A man may also be juggling multiple families in addition to multiple jobs. Finally, even worse than a father who is not available, is one who is but serves as a poor role model. Substance and physical abuse of a child's mother, the child himself, or other family members, are examples. The presence of mental and physical illnesses will factor in the quality of these interactions as well.

Further arrangements include fathers who have sole or joint custody. But, for the moment, we will be concerned with the expectations when no man is in the home, and minimally present, if at all, outside of it. For purposes of modeling, acceptable surrogates include stepfathers, uncles, grandfathers, and in rarer instances, big brothers, Babas, and coaches. Regardless, we all know that a woman can raise a boy, but a raising a **man** requires some significant male influence. The man village demands all hands on deck. Every man who is physically and mentally capable and of good moral fiber, should seek to have a positive impact on the young men in their community. Let's start with the traits necessary to be that beacon of light for boys other than those in our immediate homes.

## MAN CODE 3:1 A MAN SHOULD NOT BE TOO EAGER TO WORK WITH SOMEONE ELSE'S CHILDREN

Okay, we know this seems to contradict what was said about "all hands on deck." But any man working with the boys in his community needs to be doing so for **the right reasons**. It's already traumatic enough for a youth when there is no male influence inside the home. But even worse is when a man outside the home volunteers for this undertaking and is abusive or predatory. I wish I had a dime for every single parent who told me they stopped dating a man because, early on, he seemed too interested in her boys. This is generally a sign. What is described here is different than a teacher or coach with an established track record of male molding, asking for a parent's permission for a child whom they see has potential, to participate in a club, sport, or sponsored activity. In any event, the burden is placed on the parent to vet these situations.

In fact, there are times when, sensing the gravity of the responsibility involved, the potential mentor might be hesitant. I arrived at Man Code 3:1 quite by accident. In addition to being a public school English teacher and administrator, I served on the board of an independent school where my niece and nephew attended. We were fortunate in that this K-8 institution was a real village that annually met the state's standards for adequate yearly progress. However, one of the board's charges was expulsion hearings. A veil of sadness pervaded the process as parents would sometimes break down. These meetings were tough for the board also because our body had to vote on which children we had to let go, knowing that for our demographic, other viable options for the kids to get a quality offering were slim and none.

One parent had two children, one seven and one six, who had been written up for a litany of offenses. After the violations were cited, we were ready to vote on the fate of these young men. But out of nowhere, the mother interjected with a unique intervention. "I want **Baba Whitney** to mentor my boys!!" My mind responded with an idea of its own, '**Let's NOT do THAT!!**' Thoughts about how such a solution would interfere with my personal life flooded my brain. I also felt guilty and somewhat selfish for thinking that way. For the reasons already mentioned, my initial reluctance proved not to be a bad idea, especially since I knew I would take this kind of leadership role seriously.

My more than two-decade involvement with Demarcalin and Markenson has turned out to be one of the most enriching and rewarding experiences I have ever had. The boys' conduct improved, and they graduated from high school and later college. The brothers became upstanding citizens of the community, and, as men, are now public servants who have started families of their own. My fear that mentoring them would somehow intrude on my personal time could not have been further from the truth. I actually enjoyed the birthday parties, baseball and football games, school conferences, religious ceremonies and rights of passage, and weddings almost as much as they did!

What made everything easy is that Demarcalin and Markenson's mother had built the boat, she just needed me to help them row it! Perhaps the most gratifying part is hearing her say,

"They couldn't have done it without you, Baba," at a recent graduation. A lesson learned is that mentorship is a **conferred** status, simply pairing a child with an adult is not enough. It is up to that **young
man** to heed what their parent, guardian or mentor is teaching them.
An ancient Egyptian proverb states, "When the **student** is **ready**, the
teacher will **appear.**" Furthermore, this maxim implies that even the
right information given at the wrong time, is not useful.

Again, positive influences on one's child don't just fall from the
sky. The selection process is the **key**. It can be a daunting task for a single mother to identify this type of role model. Ann Iverson, mother
of National Basketball Association Hall of Famer Allen Iverson, was
15 which she had him. Ann witnessed a young Allen face all manner
of adversity while being hailed the top prep football **and** basketball
player in the state of Virginia, and knew his staying in Hampton was
**not** the answer. Ms. Iverson saw a way out. In Georgetown University
Hall of Fame coach John Thompson, she envisioned someone who
could "save" her son if he accepted the challenge of molding Iverson
as a member of his basketball squad.

As fate would have it, Thompson took the young prodigy
under his tutelage, and Ann Iverson's move turned out to be a brilliant one. After several years at Georgetown, Allen departed for the
NBA, and, as they say, the rest is history. But Allen Iverson must also
be credited for seizing the opportunity to sit at the feet of a legend. A
mentor has only as much influence as a mentee **confers** on him. This
means that two great ideas need to be part of the mentor's curriculum for it to be effective.

## MAN CODE 3:2 THE LESSONS OF SELF-DISCIPLINE AND DELAYED GRATIFICATION NEED TO BE TAUGHT AND LEARNED EARLY AND OFTEN

One father began wondering whether his adolescent son were being prepared for adult reality. In particular, he didn't think it was a good idea for his wife to always be giving the young man candy. But this concern was not only because of the lack of nutrients in junk food, but the message this routine sent. The dad, who owned a cleaning business said, "**I** don't get a treat **everyday.**" He started to take his son to work with him on days the boy didn't have school, hoping he would appreciate what it took for his father to take care of the family. "I wanted him to know that if a client has a problem, daddy can't just get angry. I have to be professional. I'll ask them, 'what would you like for me to do?' I want him (the son) to see that if I don't respond appropriately, I'll lose the contract, and we won't eat."

Our father of five boys would definitely agree with this approach. Why? Because, generally, "children don't pay bills, children create bills." As young men gradually start taking on some of these obligations, there are principles that can assist them with that as well.

## MAN CODE: 3:3 INITIALLY, IT'S OKAY TO FOLLOW SOMEONE ELSE'S BLUEPRINT WHILE DESIGNING YOUR OWN

A prominent attorney used his favorite jazz musician as an example of how following in another's path, can sometimes lead you to yours. The lawyer, an avid fan of the trumpeting genius Miles Davis, recalled a conversation the budding musician had with his father, a dentist, as he graduated from high school. Davis asked for and received his dad's permission to head to New York City to study at the Juilliard School of Arts. However, Miles kept the **real** motive for relocating to the Big Apple from the elder Davis. Young Miles was actually going because he was in search of his idol, legendary saxophonist Charlie Parker. Of course, Davis found him. He learned all he could while hanging with Parker, including picking up some bad habits, but, eventually, Miles' own style emerged.

This attorney drew an analogy between Davis' journey and **his** walk. At first, the lawyer wanted to be like a childhood friend a few years older who grew up in his neighborhood and was an all-state basketball player who later starred at the collegiate level. "By the time I found out I couldn't play basketball, I was halfway through college." Of course, the momentum from the future attorney's quest meant that, although his hoop dreams were frustrated, he continued to persist until he graduated from law school and became a "star" in the courtroom. This account also demonstrates that the modeling of excellence is so transcendent, its application is relevant to any professional path!

The above also highlights another fundamental truth about men in positions of influence. The lift as we climb philosophy emphasizes that, for the great, there are those who came before and those whom will follow.

## MAN CODE 3:4 BRANDISHING A TITLE AS A 'LEADER' DOES NOT MAKE YOU ONE, HAVING DISCIPLES DOES

There will be junctures along our path where we witness men who avariciously sought the big chair they eventually occupied, but were not up to the task of executing the duties associated with it. It's not hard to find these gentlemen. They will be talking about their credentials and worthiness, while sometimes embellishing certain details, as if they are still interviewing for the position. Another conversation may be about how long they have been in the position, if that, in and of itself, makes them competent.

An additional practice they will participate in is name dropping. They may mention a well-known person they worked for, only for us to later find out that the named individual, rarely, if ever, mentions them, and does not readily or proudly proclaim the braggart as an understudy. But the biggest concern here is that while incessantly reminding you they are a leader, you seldom hear of anyone who has gotten anywhere by **following** them.

Unfortunately, the field of education is teeming with men who adore a leadership title, but miss the runaway when it comes to fitting the description. Educational leaders who do so are problematic, not only because of the impact on learning outcomes, but also because their decisions often place the safety and well-being of students and staff in jeopardy. In our first case, we find a principal who implemented a divide and conquer strategy. In meetings and staff training, he would speak of unity. But in private, he would pit people against each other. Basically, once you confided in him something that could be construed as negative or derogatory, he would strategically share it with others. As a result, this would put the educators in his building in a state of constant conflict and turmoil.

If the men and women were at odds with each other, the principal thought they would be less of a threat to him, a definite sign of how insecure he was. Once all hell would break lose, this "leader" would sit back, laugh, shake his head and say something infantile like 'what are you going to do?' as if he had no idea what was happening.

One dramatic instance involved two former college basketball stars who also played professionally. Both were seeking an athletic director's position at this principal's school. On multiple occasions, the principal shared with each something unflattering he claimed they said about the other, and gleefully watched these two large gentlemen almost come to blows. Such behavior is the total antithesis of the Man Code, since real men don't create drama, they squash it!

In studies of alpha male gorillas, it was found that the primates' lofty status among their peers came, not necessarily through exhibitions of brute strength, but from primarily two skills—their ability to be **empathetic**, and their knack for conflict **resolution**. The type of leaders we are currently discussing, do exactly the opposite by muddying the waters and creating dissension in place of peace and harmony.

Our father of five boys, an auto worker by trade, shared a proverb which contrasts the leadership style in the case above, with a more appropriate one. **"God's math is addition and multiplication. Satan's is subtraction and division."** Thus, even though our divide and conquer leader grew up in, attended school, and was a veteran in the district where he was employed, there was very little positive or inspiring that those in this community said about him. He was known as a pathological liar whose only example was a poor one. Not one youth or former graduate said they learned anything of value or achieved any of their goals or aspirations as a result of his guidance or counsel.

I find such a scenario almost an achievement itself, since even a broken clock is right twice a day. There are two additional male principals I would like to add to the leaders without disciples category. Their examples only vary in the particulars. Both threw out big names in the district they worked in and boasted about their relationship with them. Upon further review, we found the two wildly exaggerated their connection to these "mentors" to make themselves look good, or, their interaction with them was minimal at best. Meanwhile, their more seasoned and accomplished peers, who were also principals, saw them as "a-- kissers" or "stupid," an opinion often shared by the principals' staffs.

Such depictions are common among these types of leaders since, as the old saying goes, "incompetence breeds loyalty." This meant that those hired on their administrative teams were cronies or women they were having sex with. Now let us set the record straight. As men, we all have faults and flaws, and are all creatures of the flesh. So I would never suggest that a leader should hire people they have no familiarity with or don't trust! Furthermore, I would also never argue that we have problems with supervisors merely because they are involved in a workplace affair, especially since we're dealing with adults, and these events are commonplace. However, we **do** expect everyone to **do their jobs**. When they don't, these items are issues!

Therefore, the principals of record, who in their vanity fancied themselves as ladies men, ended up having their lives threatened and being extorted as a result of their "after school specials." These circumstances compromised the safety of the children and adults in their buildings because the animosity directed toward them was brought to the school campuses!

Again, the three principals above did not avail themselves to successful role models. Unfortunately, the life of a leader does not always allow do-overs. It's too late to ask for an elder statesman's advice, when, as happened to one of the principals, a student dies on your watch, and your building is the subject of a district and law enforcement investigation into his death as a possible murder.

The only real accomplishment of the leadership style we're describing is drama 24/7. Furthermore, since these leaders were so insecure, they surrounded themselves with staff and leadership team members whose credentials and intelligence weren't threatening to their own. Finally, anyone following these three couldn't have claimed to have gotten anywhere, because you are who you are around, and the model they exemplified was one of incompetence and dysfunction.

On the other end of the spectrum, let's examine two men who actually made the people around them **better**. In our first case, the attorney we previously discussed, yes, the one who used Miles Davis and a local star athlete to fuel his ascent to prominence, began his practice with some childhood friends in his hometown. After an inauspicious beginning, he gradually built his firm into one that represented a diverse clientele. Professional athletes and entertainers took their place alongside the working people and those who got expert representation for free. But being the senior partner in a law firm is no walk in the park. As associates left to become judges and start their own practices, our lawyer had to make sure his overhead was covered and business continued as usual.

This was part of the plan. He told every attorney who joined, he was there to train and support them, but not hold their hand. The senior partner expected these rising stars to spread their wings, and, at some point, hang their own shingles. That's exactly what happened. Decades later, a local newspaper had a photo of the lawyers that passed through his firm. Nearly 30 were in the picture, and this still wasn't all of them. There were those who couldn't make it. The actual number was closer to 100!

Of course, the former partners, through deeds and words, have never stopped expressing the gratitude they felt for the opportunity to train under their fearless leader.

A second and well-known case of how a rising tide can lift all sails, is the brilliant business acumen of Percy Miller, also known as Master P. Before leaving his hometown of New Orleans, Louisiana to build his recording label on the West Coast, Miller made a stop at the University of Houston, where he was a business major. One day while doing some research, Miller read a statistic that grabbed his attention. He saw that pop music legend Michael Jackson received 80% of his publishing.

Miller was intrigued. He found the number for Jackson's legal counsel and set up a meeting. Although the lawyer charged him an exorbitant fee for the advice, Miller used the information to establish his own recording empire. The goal was full ownership, not an arrangement that made him and his artists permanently indebted to someone else's label. The No Limit Records CEO became a game changer, not just because of the company's commercial success, but also because of the autonomy he gave to his performers.

Miller envisioned his entertainers being able to stand on their own two feet. Unlike other CEO's who were obsessed with controlling their talent, Miller insisted that anyone with No Limit put the cars they were driving and homes they were living in in **their** name. In addition, he encouraged them to start their own **businesses** so they could maintain their independence! Artists appreciated how magnanimous Miller was. For some, it was an opportunity to focus on making music and not worry about escaping death threats. In addition, after meeting their obligations to the label, there were those who left No Limit owning the publishing rights to their music, which is virtually unheard of.

Remember, the Man Code asks anyone calling themselves a general, 'where is your army?'

While the school leaders in our study would have to answer with silence, Miller's No Limit Army was his artists, our attorney's was the legion of lawyers trained at his firm. Both men also have something to say about the mindset needed to make money.

## MAN CODE 3:5 'YOU CAN'T BE SCARED AND MAKE NO MONEY'

Millionaires Row was far from a primrose path for Miller and our lawyer. The path to glory is full of obstructions and road blocks, and overcoming them is what distinguishes the champion from those whom merely fall by the wayside. In the case of the attorney, his commitment to providing quality counsel to all and promoting social justice, meant that, on multiple occasions, he received death threats and his law firm was shot up. When asked did this deter him? our lawyer responded, 'you can't be **scared** and make no money!'

Miller would probably agree. When word got out that he moved his fledgling recording company and artists to the West Coast to set up shop, he got "the call." A well-known mogul from another label suggested that Miller should rethink relocating to the area. Miller's response was that he had already bought a home and wasn't planning on going anywhere. In fact, Miller said if the town were too big for the both of them, perhaps **he should** leave. Although not used to rejection, the mogul learned Miller meant business—he stayed in California!

You may have noticed that a man's journey to independence, prosperity and self-definition can be rough. Where we go to seek wisdom and guidance can be critical. Your network is the key! Thus, through good times and bad, the maintenance of one's Man Circle is essential. We close this chapter by studying these relationships and their value in our continued development and well-being.

## MAN CODE 3:6 EVERY NOW AND THEN, A MAN'S TEAM NEEDS TO CLOSE THE LOCKER ROOM DOOR AND HOLD A 'PLAYER'S ONLY MEETING'

"For the strength of the Pack is the Wolf, and the strength of the Wolf is the Pack," is a quote from Rudyard Kipling cited everywhere from English classes to championship-winning coaches. As we stated before, you are whom you are around. In this section, we will examine the occasions when we as men must convene in order to receive the psychological, spiritual, and social support essential to our survival. In other words, we must use this opportunity to convince the award-winning coach discussed in Chapter Two, it's time to exit his restroom, get out of the house and hang out with the fellas for a moment.

You may wonder what constitutes the kind of gathering we are discussing. The event is not as important as the opportunity for male bonding. The attorney in the previous example, went golfing and played tennis with the guys for diversion. He even bought a ranch so his friends and their families could swim, play basketball and ride horses and motorcycles, among other activities. Percy Miller was a basketball player, so it was nothing to find him on the court engaged in a competitive game of hoops with his label mates when he wasn't in the board room or studio. Sports are excellent outlets because they relieve stress, and promote physical fitness while also fortifying the Man Network.

Of course, as mentioned above, the relief of stressors related to family, career, and interpersonal issues, is critical to healthy male functioning. But there will be times when we will need to get serious topics "off our chest" and search for answers to life's dilemmas. In these moments, the Man Code insists we be fast listeners and slow advisers for our friends and comrades. Although our circles may not include actual therapists—we can all learn something from them: be a good listener.

Sometimes if you let a man pour his heart out, the solution to his problems may emerge organically. If prompted to give advice, a good policy is to make sure you are qualified before opening your mouth. Think of the consequences! There is nothing wrong with saying you don't know, or referring your friend to someone else, inside or **outside** the Circle. Often, the best advice is none!

A National Basketball Association Hall of Famer who won multiple championships, use to open up his cavernous lakeside estate to other athletes. Current and former college and professional basketball and football players made sure they took advantage of this icon's hospitality whenever the call went out. They were there to see each other in addition to soak up the wisdom of the home's occupant. A frequent visitor was a brash young star still playing in the NBA, who has won multiple championships himself. Of course, his conversation was different from the old man's, who was generally reserved and, instead of talking about sports, would listen to his young visitors or address trending news stories or world affairs.

The young buck, who was adjusting to his newfound wealth after emerging from a challenging economic background, loved to mention how much he paid for his jewelry, clothes and cars. One day, the Hall of Famer was asked privately why he didn't suggest that the young man should be more modest. The old man responded, **"You know I would never tell another man how to spend his money."**

But regardless of the excuse, bowling, a game of cards, watching the game, home improvement and construction, community service, or an impromptu rap session, when possible, we should share positive energy and be in good spirits. When I discussed how much I enjoyed the comradery of some of the fellas at a gym where I work out, a friend said, "you sound like a kid." I told her that I took that as a compliment. A man can never get his childhood back, but he can exploit the release of endorphins that comes from physically emptying the bucket during a challenging workout. The opportunity to fellowship with his brethren in the process, is a bonus!

A neighbor, who is retired, has a pool table in his home, yet insists on venturing out to shoot billiards at a pool hall in the area, despite the fact his buddies show him no mercy. Why? Because for my neighbor, the outcome of the contests is beside the point. The real win is the chance to enjoy the company of old friends. His buddies, however, are okay with the fact he won't present much of a challenge. "They'd be disappointed if I didn't show up," my neighbor said laughing. "They would probably call the police to make sure I'm okay."

We should never underestimate the role that esprit de corps plays in establishing a winning culture. This value is an indispensable element if we are to continue to perform effectively through good times and bad. The young man at the beginning of the chapter was named the Associated Press Basketball Coach of the Year in his state. If he has one lesson for us as he resurfaces from the quiet of his study, it's that a team must operate as one. Tough practices were one tool he used to bring his squad together. "Sometimes, they would all be mad at me. That's okay, as long as they were **unified.**"

## MAN CODE 3:7 MAY THE CIRCLE BE UNBROKEN (STRATEGIES FOR MAINTENANCE OF THE MAN CIRCLE)

When I solicited ideas for the topics this essay would examine, a participant asked me to discuss reciprocity. In particular, he loaned a friend some money and he made sure it wasn't an amount that would hurt him, because the friend (somebody I know) had a track record of not paying the funds back. My question to him was is this something that **he** practices? In other words, does he always return the money he receives from his benefactors?

Because I know the answer is no, I want him to see the irony— why are you so adamant that others follow rules that you don't? Let's be clear, I'm not condoning anyone not respecting an agreement. However, the Code is unambiguous regarding such matters: we must practice **THE GOLDEN RULE.** Do unto others as you would have them to do unto you, and stop expecting of your peers that which they cannot expect from you! Maybe if we set a better example, others would have one to follow.

Everything covered in this section is inspired by the golden rule. The three factors of circle maintenance are time, money, and respect. Although time and money are big rooms, they are subsumed in the mansion of respect. The rule is that we must dip our brushes in gold if the walls are to be painted properly. Friends may enter, but they may stay only if they observe the house rules. Since we got the ball rolling with money, let's address that first.

In a perfect world, a great policy to adhere to is neither a lender nor a borrower be. But because our bonds are based on needing something from each other, that item might be funds. The Code is to honor any repayment agreement in kind. If you are loaned money under the pretense you will pay it back, unless otherwise mutually agreed upon, you must compensate the lender with actual money. How would you feel, if when you needed funds, the giver said, "Instead of that, how about if I come over and babysit your kids tomorrow, or give you a ride to work?" At some point those might be fine, but that's not **what you asked for!**

Next, a lender knows when he has been paid back. Doing things in secret, like letting your friend spend the night when they are in town, or paying for dinner once in a while, things you probably should be doing anyway, don't count, unless they did that for you and expected to be paid back in that manner.

If you can't pay back the money, or can't return it in full and require some kind of arrangement, then say so. Sometimes people think if they can't remunerate the lender, somehow the problem will disappear. In actuality, your partner hasn't forgotten. They may have lost respect for you or think you don't care.

The inability to communicate properly when such conflicts surface can fracture a friendship and cause irreparable harm. Again, remember how you would feel if it were you. When you are repaying the funds, you aren't doing them a favor, you are keeping your word and salvaging some semblance of dignity and respect. You are doing this for **yourself** as much as the donor. Furthermore, don't harbor immature thoughts like 'they don't need it,' or 'they seem to be doing alright, they'll be okay (without it).' Who are we to determine what other people need their money for? What if they took the stance you didn't need it when you asked for it?

Time like land, is such an invaluable resource, because we can't make more of it. Of all the elements, time is perhaps the most critical, because it's the only thing we can't regain once it is lost. Money is somewhat different, and the people in this study know it. You can build an empire, lose it, and by applying the principles in the Man Code, rebuild. But you can't get time back, thus it is of the essence that we don't waste it. Require of your fellows that they stay on the clock, and make sure you do as well.

There is an old saying: if you're early, you're on time, if you're on time, you're late, and if you are late, that is unacceptable. With nearly everyone having personal communication devices at their disposal with alarms, planners, and the works, there is only one excuse for being late: an actual emergency. There is nothing wrong with calling in advance to alter the plan, or saying you can't make it. But a no-show, no-call is unacceptable. The unseen side is that when someone is depending on you to be on time, you may be creating an emergency because of all the people who depend on them!

Just as we need to ask who are we to determine how bad others need their money, we should ask ourselves the same question regarding others' time. In the military being punctual is not an option—it's a matter of life and death. Demarcalin, who was mentioned earlier in the essay, learned to become very efficient during basic training for the Army. When the cadets were awakened each morning at 4:30 a.m., they had **15** minutes to fix their bed, shower and get dressed. However, Demarcalin and a few fellow trainees learned how to "game" the system. They were on Code. Instead of waiting for their superiors, they woke themselves up and got started in advance.

Champions know it is a great idea to be available and ready ahead of schedule because doing so reduces stress and assists you in getting more accomplished. A not so secret practice of many employers is to chart when prospective hires arrive for an interview. They know the way you start will be how you will finish. If a recruit doesn't show up in a timely fashion when they have yet to secure the position, what will be the incentive once they do?

Punctuality is also a key in performance training. This is particularly true in systems where groups have high expectations, and therefore, demand more from each individual. In 1981, Indiana University's basketball team planned to compete for an NCAA championship. Forward Landon Turner complained to guard Isiah Thomas, the team's leader, that the ball was not being passed to him enough during games. "I'm not passing you the ball in a game unless I see it in practice," Thomas replied. Indeed, that level of trust resulted in IU winning the title that year.

With respect to circle maintenance, we have already stated, most items involving time and financial integrity, have the issue of respect embedded. For example, a member of our circle consistently came to us upset about issues in his domestic life. He was given *sound* advice from one who *knew* how to handle such matters. As we have said in 3:6, not everyone is qualified. But this gentleman was, he had already fought that fire. However, the complainant chose not to follow the instructions given and thought the circle would support his persistent crying about the adversity he was experiencing.

We felt our time was not being respected, not to mention the emotional and psychological toll these rants were inflicting on us. *We had our **own** problems.* The circle is for good men who may be going through hell. It is not for those who post up in the inferno and then later want sympathy for their third-degree burns. We are solution-oriented. You don't have to listen to the circle. But you're not going to ignore us and keep bringing the same topics back. This gentleman lost his seat at the table.

Sometimes you have to love your brother from afar. But alas, all was not lost! Even though it took an incubation period, the information finally resonated with the young man. Years later, he has gotten his act together and begun anew. He now expresses gratitude for the coaching he received during this period, because it aided him in working through the crisis. We *get* it. Let the circle say amen!

Although we all could use some "straightening" every now and then, we should not be needier or more high maintenance than what members in the circle have going on at work, home, or other aspects of their personal life. As a man, you learn to persevere. The whole purpose of a training room is to get the athlete back ready to play, you don't find home in there!

Respect also means not being disparaging or covetous of what other men have, financial or otherwise. Resentment generally is the outcome when you could have done better but didn't for some reason. That's nobody's fault but yours! A man has to see that it is within himself to have whatever life or lifestyle that he desires. Proclaiming, providing and protecting is what we do. In fact, in Chapter Four, we go from the vision to its realization.

But let's not get ahead of ourselves. A paraprofessional in the school system was once part of the tribe. One of his favorite disclaimers was, "I wish I could afford that. But I can't because I don't make the same salary as the teachers." What's funny is that even though I was the only teacher present, and because my energy was in a more positive space, I thought the comment was directed at teachers in general, **not me**. In addition, I was not used to a teacher's salary being the envy of other professionals. I guess there are levels.

Despite this, the paraprofessional made the statement on multiple occasions. Although I didn't feel it was a personal jab, others did. "Why don't you go to school and get a teaching certificate like Woods?" one friend asked. Silence. That was the last we heard of the comment. We should never covet what others have, especially since we may not know or may not be willing to do what they had to do to get it.

For instance, the attorney featured in this work, would be the frequent subject of jealous remarks of people in his community. But most of them were not made to his face, which was a good thing since many knew they might need him. However, few asked themselves if **they** were capable of putting in the work necessary to achieve the prominence and prosperity reserved for the elite? It's not likely. Most would probably get fatigued just thinking about the kind of time and effort demanded to attain such an envied status!

On the other side, there are people who only want to be surrounded by friends who have less than them, so they can be the leader of their pack. We have one word for those in this category: insecure. Such thinking is like intelligence. It is said that if you are the smartest guy in the room, you're in the wrong room. There are those who don't want to be challenged. We have a word for them too: losers!

Another box we have to tick off in the respect category, is respect for another man's woman. We touched on some of this in Chapter Two, but it's not just deeds, some things are better left unsaid. Once more, we will employ the golden rule. Some of the most habitual line steppers are men who would not want their significant others looked at in such a manner.

Once a celebration was held at a friend's house for a man who was to be married for a second time. The only female present was the wife of the host. Although petite, she was athletic and was wearing a pair of blue jean shorts. On one occasion, she passed through the living room, and the host's buddy, a childhood friend, said something about how good she looked in the shorts. Of course, the host wasn't in the room at the time. Interestingly enough, the wife of the man talking was not exactly a painted pony. We tried to imagine him appreciating someone making a similar statement about his wife. We couldn't.

Finally, a lot of the business shared in the circle members should expect to stay in the circle. But what does the playbook stipulate regarding a personal item disseminated between members about another? The father of five boys said, "If it's not something that you would feel comfortable saying with that person in the room, it's probably not a good idea to bring it up."

The necessity for the exercise of discretion in the circle is an excellent lesson for us to close our chapter on "Modeling, Mentoring and Male Bonding." Before we move on, let's review the content covered. We introduced mentoring as the coaching process for young men to gain access to the perspectives and experience needed to be considered a man. Although this is a call to arms in the man village, there are some arms we do not need wrapped around our children, for obvious reasons. Two key concepts boys should learn along their journey are self-discipline and delayed gratification.

Moreover, there's nothing wrong with using the models of the great, as you create your own. In addition, every great leader has someone exemplary in front of as well as behind them, when "leaders" don't, their only legacy will be calamity. We also emphasized that prosperity and fearlessness go hand in hand, and that male bonding is an essential component of ongoing male development and survival. Furthermore, we analyzed the three components of circle maintenance. Membership has its privileges because we honor each other's time, money, and respect.

What follows is an analysis of excellence in diverse disciplines, men who dared to be great and the traits that defined them. During a practice, a major college basketball coach expressed his disdain at the team's lack of effort by blowing the whistle and bringing a drill to a screeching halt. He exploded. **"If you do what everybody else is doing, you will have what everybody else has!!"** The examples you will see next, were able to separate themselves from the pack for that precise reason: they weren't 'doing what everyone else' was doing!

# CHAPTER FOUR:

## *Coming Early And Staying Late*

**For the artists, athletes,** entertainers, entrepreneurs, scholars, veterans, and others in this part of the essay, a journey of a thousand miles began with the first step, and their first step, was creating a vision of the possible. The creative process is mental. Part of it is what scientists call "having a model of the problem."

As a student attending Pontiac (Michigan) High School, the late A. Alfred Taubman was considered to be "slow." In today's parlance, he would have been identified as "special needs." But while selling shoes in downtown Pontiac, there was something he wondered about. He wanted to know what stores without doors would look like. Taubman was committed to finding out. The United States' largest builder of malls, started his billion-dollar empire with a loan from his father. Later, Taubman would own a significant stake in Sotheby's, the world's largest auction house.

Some describe a vision as beginning with the ending. Artists draw outlines and fill in, and so do writers; this chapter began with a few notes. If a man doesn't know where he is going, how in the world is he going to get there? Aumon was an honors graduate student. Before the first session of each class, Aumon would introduce himself to his professors and inform them he planned on getting an A, and wanted them to let him know what he needed to do to accomplish this goal. The result was a master's degree and, of course, a 4.0 average. He also passed this wisdom down to his son, whom we will discuss later.

In the seminal treatise *The Art of War*, Sun Tzu states, "Therefore, a victorious army first wins and then seeks battle." We will now turn our attention to preparation and its role in securing the desired outcome for the gentlemen below. It should come as no surprise that for these men to become elite in their respective fields of endeavor, they had to exhibit a drive and work ethic not evident in their peers. A vision may jump start a dream, but having a mountain in your sights and scaling it are two different things.

## MAN CODE 4:1 YOU ARE WHAT YOU CONSISTENTLY DO

Long before he made it to New York City and began his legendary run as one of the greatest jazz musicians in the world, as previously noted, Miles Davis was a kid who grew up in southern Illinois. Once, a cousin of Miles was talking about her childhood and what life was like in Alton, a small town. She described Davis as a hermit. The cousin said she rarely, if ever, saw him. "We could hear him though. He was always upstairs in his room playing his trumpet."

Upon his arrival in California, Percy Miller knew it would not take long for his No Limit Records to develop their niche in the music industry. For Miller, it was okay for the other labels to be conspicuous for their partying. No Limit cornered the market with its non-stop work ethic. A member of Miller's creative team, a group of producers collectively known as Beats by the Pound, was in the studio practically 24 hours seven days a week. The impressive volume of music No Limit produced during this period speaks for itself.

The prominent attorney we've been discussing did not start out that way. In the formative years, he and his partners had to do a lot of ripping and running in order to make ends meet. On more than a few occasions, this made him late for proceedings. The lawyers on the other side, mostly prosecutors, tried to take advantage of the situation by requesting dismissals.

However, the judges, for the most part, understood. They respected the fact that our lawyer had a smaller firm and had to work harder and take on more cases to pay the firm's bills, and the jurists weren't afraid to inform the prosecutors of these facts. The opposing attorneys groaned, waited grudgingly, and once the man of the hour appeared, lost another case to him! Beyond this maverick lawyer's creativity, and nearly encyclopedic command of case law, what struck fear in the hearts of those who opposed him, was his incessant drive and relentless pursuit of victory.

As in the above case, where the judges granted the attorney some leeway, your peers and even your detractors will acknowledge a man who demonstrates an uncompromising work ethos. Respect and recognition are the currency of a sustained commitment to excellence, regardless of one's calling. It generally takes years to develop such a high level of functioning. But once again, this progression will not occur unless you are exposed to the right models!

I met Jim and Stan while I was pursuing my bachelor's degree. They were in graduate school. However, I was not a serious student and my fellowship with them had more to do with the desire to play basketball and hang out. They had cars and I didn't. I was a journalism major who was doing just enough to maintain a " C" average, being an honor student was not a priority since I was jealousy guarding my "free time." I soon learned that though Jim and Stan were also interested in enjoying themselves, they did so only after they had completed their studies.

I thought that everyone was on the same program I was. I was wrong. There were afternoons that I called Stan as soon as I got home from class. I was asking if he could pick me up to go hoop or to a club in town. Sometimes he answered in the affirmative and we would have a great time. Other times, he would respond with, "Whit, I have a paper I have to write," or, "I have a test tomorrow." I was baffled. Maybe I believed **everyone** was doing the bare minimum to get by.

Jim's approach wasn't much different than his friend Stan's. One weekend, I invited him to spend a night over my grandparents' house, where I was living while going to school. He brought his typewriter. That Friday night, I carried on a conversation with Jim as he sat at the dining room table working on a paper. As Friday evening turned into early Saturday morning, I told Jim I was retreating to my room in the basement. I reminded him that he could crash on the living room couch.

At about 9 or 10 that morning, I emerged from my slumber in the basement expecting Jim to be on the couch sleep. Instead, he was still at the table. I asked him did he get any rest? "Naw, man, basically, I was up all night working on this paper." Jim's tireless effort in completing his work left such an indelible impression on me, that nearly 40 years later, the image of him sitting there typing, is still etched in my brain.

The lesson that Jim and Stan inadvertently taught me through their examples was a simple one: there's a time for everything. Their discipline paid off. Jim went on to obtain a law degree from Northwestern University and Stan got a doctorate of dentistry from the University of North Carolina. What Jim did is reminiscent of a piece of advice NBA All-Star Dwight Howard received when he was in high school.

Howard played in Hall of Famer Michael Jordan's Jordan Brand Classic high school all-star game. Howard, who was forgoing college to play in the league, took full advantage of this opportunity to pick the brain of a legend. Howard asked Jordan how he could get better. Jordan didn't mince words. "You have to practice while your opponent is sleeping."

When asked what his secret was to being an honors student at the graduate level, Aumon provided each day's itinerary. Aumon had a job at a food bank that he used to help support his wife, a teacher, and his young son. He said he would study in the morning before work. Then, Aumon would study again during his lunch break. A third session would follow that night before going to bed.

Pete, a retired pilot for American Airlines, received his bachelor's degree from the Air Force Academy and a Master's in Business Administration from the University of California at Berkeley. Pete said one thing he learned in his pursuit of academic and professional excellence is, "When you get **there**, you find out its not that many people who really **want** it."

## MAN CODE 4:2 WHEN YOUR NUMBER IS CALLED, YOU HAVE TO BE READY

The title of this section is a famous saying of Hall of Fame NBA Coach and Executive Pat Riley. In the NBA, depth may help you get through the regular season, but the playoffs are different. In the playoffs, where every game is critical, the rotation is tighter, and a team may only play seven or eight men. Thus, players six through eight can make a difference. Another way of looking at this is Riley is saying the reserves have to be prepared once they enter the game off the bench. A man must jump at an opportunity when it presents itself, because one never knows if or when there will be an encore.

Darrin, Aumon's only son, is the embodiment of the kind of preparedness Riley spoke of. As a high school student, Darrin wanted to make some extra money, so he asked his parents if he could work. He was flat out rejected. "Your job is school," his mother said. Darrin's goal was to attend the University of Michigan. His aspirations seemed within reach since he applied the lessons of hard work learned from his parents to become an honor student himself. However, Darrin's counselor, Mr. Graham, who was notorious for killing students' dreams, tried to steer the young man in another direction.

Graham was pushing his alma mater. "You ought to go to Central Michigan University," he kept telling Darrin. Of course, by his senior year, Darrin was accepted to Michigan, and other top-notch schools were beginning to show interest. Darrin assumed he was going to Michigan, but kept his options open. When representatives from Harvard University came to the area, Darrin attended the informational session.

Harvard's recruiters provided all in attendance with a checklist of what they needed to do if they were interested in being considered for admission. Darrin vowed to complete each task. Meanwhile, the naysayers that surfaced seemed worse than Mr. Graham. They told Darrin that Harvard wasn't going to accept a student from an ordinary public school in a factory town. Darrin ignored them while trying not to get his hopes up too high. When Darrin was accepted to Northwestern University, he was intrigued enough that he wanted to visit the campus.

There was only one problem. Aumon, Darrin's father and an inspiration for his excellent scholarship, would not be taking him. He passed away before Darrin's senior year. An uncle took him instead. Darrin was blown away by the trip. On the return home from Evanston, Darrin said, "Uncle Tee, I think I know where I will be spending my next four years."

Darrin thought his visit to Northwestern solidified his choice of a college, without realizing the final chapter had yet to be written. Apparently, Harvard has a habit of informing students of its decisions late in their senior year, and that is when Darrin found out he was accepted. It's too bad Aumon didn't live to see his son get into Harvard. He would have been proud!

For Darrin and his mother, the decision was a no-brainer: he was headed to Cambridge, Massachusetts. Darrin puts his Harvard degree to good use as a teacher and mentor at an elite international school. Darrin would tell anyone reading how heeding all of the items on Harvard's admissions checklist improved his life chances. His case is a brilliant illustration of how opportunity rewards those who are prepared.

A tireless work ethic and constant preparation for the chances that will inevitably define a man's legacy, are two traits of high-end performers. There are several more. From here, the battle gets increasingly mental and the road narrower. Warning to reader: we will be raising the intensity and level of difficulty of the analysis. At this point, we have readied and aimed, now it is time to **FIRE!**

## MAN CODE 4:3 TRUST IN YOUR PREPARATION

A woman who was from a long suffering college football fan base, asked the new coach of her favorite university how long it would take for his team to defeat their hated rival. "Sixty minutes," he said. We must ask ourselves, what's the point of all that preparation if we're not confident enough to put it to good use? Would it have made sense for Michael Talley to dominate against grown men on the weekends, and then be scared against his peers in a high school basketball game? How logical would it have been for our attorney to escape death threats only to go into a court of law and be intimidated by an "opposing argument?" Sounds silly doesn't it?

While these two scenarios may appear ridiculous, it is not uncommon to see men fail, even those who are professionals, when they do not trust in their preparation. Mark Johnson is a former math teacher and a veteran of the Gulf War in Iraq. Johnson said he and others in his unit spent countless hours drilling on how to put on their gear. One member appeared to be particularly confident in this as well as other areas of his training.

However, one day the sound of enemy fire could be heard exploding in the distance and it was time to get ready. Johnson said the young soldier started trembling and experienced difficulties getting his equipment on. "I couldn't help him because I had to put my own stuff on. The first thing you're taught in the military, is to take care of yourself first."

Why would you spend your entire life getting ready for a moment, only to run from it? Mario, an attorney in Florida, said he was dumbfounded by the behavior of some of his classmates in law school. "Many of them wouldn't even show up for their final exams because they were afraid they were going to fail. I figured, they have already got my money, at least I got to take a shot at it."

In the case of Jack Nicklaus, he expected to do more than "take a shot at it." Nicklaus, the current record holder for Professional Golf Association major tournament wins with 18, always felt he had a great chance to prevail. He said at most tournaments, he could eliminate at least half the field, because they "didn't **think** they could win."

The late great UCLA basketball coach John Wooden, who won 10 NCAA championships, felt his teams were so well prepared that by game time, "I could have taken a nap." Like Wooden, we must learn to approach each challenge with a sense of resignation, giving ourselves to the moment and letting the chips fall where they may.

A favorite saying of coaches once their week of preparation for a game is complete is, "The hay is in the barn." There are even those who say the only time you're nervous is when you are not prepared. Perhaps one reason for a warrior's confidence is that he knows he has turned every stone in his quest for excellence.

## MAN CODE 4:4 THE HIGHER THE LEVEL OF COMPETITION, THE LESS THE MARGIN OF ERROR

In life, there will always be levels. For instance, there's youth, amateur, collegiate, and professional. There are also distinctions within levels. For example, you may have apprentices and semi-professionals. Even among professionals, there is a separate category for the elite. During this discussion, we will delve into the minds of those who have distinguished themselves in their respective occupations.

A former assistant coach in the National Football League once said he agrees that while most Hollywood portrayals of pro football fall short, *Any Given Sunday* has a scene that comes the closest. In a rousing pep talk to his team, the coach, played by Al Pacino, drops a gem, according to the former coach. "It's a game of **inches,** and the inches are **everywhere.**" At the professional level, most games come down to a play or two. In addition to offense and defense, an advantage can be gained on special teams.

When a coach who has won multiple championships was asked what's the difference between teams who are able to make plays in crucial situations and those that aren't? he said a team will play harder if players feel a coach cares about them as a person. At the collegiate level, this may mean, "asking a kid how his family is doing, or how school is going?" the coach said. However, this approach may seem counter-intuitive in the pros, since they are considered to be more of a business.

While professional coaches can insist on an athlete doing "his job" and letting him know if he needs a friend to "get a dog," there are ways pro coaches can show some love too, according to this coach. He pointed to one who has won multiple NBA championships, who demonstrates his appreciation by regularly picking up the tabs for his players at expensive restaurants at home and on the road.

This gesture is generally well received not because the players, most of whom are millionaires and get per diems anyway, can't afford to feed themselves, rather, it's the thought that counts! Obviously, these same points could probably be applied to the corporate world. In his *The Art of War*, for example, Sun Tzu addresses the advantages of treating "the soldiers" well.

In gaining "the inches," as men we can never allow ourselves to get complacent and forget about the human dynamic. Terry, who owns a moving company, said the quality of his service is not the only factor that will determine whether he gets repeat business. He must maintain a professional demeanor at all times. "It takes years to get a customer, but only seconds to lose one."

Even in large corporations, attending to details is key. Nearly one hundred years ago, a famous study was done at a Western Electric plant in Hawthorne, a suburb of Chicago, Illinois. The factory's managers wanted to know what effect lighting would have on worker productivity. They increased the lighting and output increased. The lighting was decreased and an increase was still observed. Finally, it was clear that the lighting wasn't what lead to an uptick in productivity. The researchers concluded that the mere fact that management was paying attention to the workers, lead to the changes noted.

The value of "paying attention" to those in your employ can be an asset in other fields as well. Sometimes, cultural differences can influence production models and thereby create an **edge** for a competitor. Although Asian automakers have been making automobiles for more than a century, they were not on the radar of North American car producers until the 1970's. By then, Asian companies began to master the techniques of mass production they learned from their Western counterparts, and created market segmentation by building cheaper and more fuel efficient vehicles. But the icing on the cake was when they started churning out more **reliable** cars.

This trend continued despite the fact that Free Trade Agreements meant American manufacturers were producing cars in Asia and Asian firms built cars in the West. But regardless of where the carriages were constructed, there remained a vast difference in philosophy. While the West was still heavily reliant on specialization and division of labor, Asian automakers became known for a teaming concept which created a tighter nexus between automotive designers and management, and the labor ultimately responsible for producing the vehicles.

The feedback loop was also unique. As opposed to the more top-down structure of the American automakers, Asian assemblers' input was more valued and even encouraged. The thinking behind this was two-fold: a higher quality product and a more engaged employee. Wooden would definitely agree with the importance of leaders listening to those in their charge because, "the players have brains too."

In any field, there is always an advantage in the knowledge that the **whole** must be greater than the sum total of its parts. As with the Asian automakers, anytime frontline workers actually see how their efforts contribute to the finished product, an employer gets a heads up on its rivals. Perhaps this is why in the corporate world, those who move from the mail room to the board room, can offer more practical, efficient and more worker-friendly solutions to organizational challenges, than someone who has merely risen from middle management.

But while seeking to perform at optimal levels in our professional lives, we must not neglect the little things, namely the **fundamentals.** We can all relate to a basketball player who is so excited to enter the game for the first time, he forgets to check in at the scorer's table. As in all facets of life though, the novelty wears off and we improve through repetition.

Coach Wooden made sure his first instruction to players at the beginning of each season, had nothing to do with x's and o's. He taught them how to put their socks on straight so they wouldn't get blisters. The coach also let his team know he did not want them drinking cold water, since it might upset their stomachs. Room temperature was fine.

Even after scrutiny of the finer points, victory is never assured. A champion knows that he is only considered such because he has competed against the best. The example of Muhammad Ali discussed in the first chapter, shows us that to be great, our opponents must be worthy and victory is meaningless without a real challenge.

The 1980's is arguably the greatest decade of NBA basketball because of the iconic rivalries between the Detroit Pistons, Los Angeles Lakers, Boston Celtics, Philadelphia Seventy Sixers, and Chicago Bulls franchises. In 1981, the Celtics were matched up against the Seventy Sixers in the Eastern Conference Finals. The Seventy Sixers had a 3-2 lead and were looking to close out the series in game six. But future Hall of Famer Celtic Kevin McHale just barely deflected a shot attempt by Andrew Toney during a key possession near the end of the game to stave off elimination for Boston.

"It's crazy when you play that hard and it comes down to a finger touching the ball," McHale said. The Celtics then won game seven of the series and went on to claim the NBA championship that year. But four years later, in 1985, the Celtics would be tested again, this time against the Lakers whom had never beaten them in the finals.

Riley, who coached the Lakers, was typical of the combatants in this rivalry. He had a nearly fanatical drive to succeed that was bolstered by practice and game-day regiments and routines which were virtually set in stone. One of Riley's rules was that only players, coaches and team staff could ride on the bus en route to a game. But one difference between champions and also-rans is their ability to exercise discretion and know when to back off. Riley's Hall of Fame Center Kareem Abdul-Jabaar had been embarrassed in the series and asked his coach for a special favor before one critical contest: would Riley allow Kareem's father to ride the bus with the team on the way to the game?

Of course, Riley said yes and Kareem's performance was vital as the Lakers went on to win the 1985 championship. Years later, Riley would comment that he was not concerned about "enforcing a **stupid rule**" when it was clear that the player who went by the nickname "The Captain," needed his father's "support."

As we stated earlier, even if one follows all of the steps previously highlighted, victory is never guaranteed. A true champion is mindful that just as he may emerge victorious, when the competition is fierce, the prospect of defeat is ever-present. Therefore, all we are really fighting for is the **opportunity.** Regardless of outcome, however, one thing is for certain. In this chapter on male performance factors, we can not avoid the inevitable, sacrifice.

## MAN CODE 4:5 EVERYBODY WANTS TO GO TO HEAVEN, BUT NOBODY WANTS TO DIE

A price is paid and a toll is exacted every time men "step between the lines" of their respective undertakings. In economics, this phenomenon is similar to "opportunity cost," where you compare the advantages of the time and effort expended in one area to other options. For example, if Miles Davis had stayed at the Juilliard School of the Arts instead of pursuing his idol Charlie Parker, we might have had a music teacher instead of one of the greatest trumpeters ever!

In Man Code 4:1 "You are what you consistently do," it was firmly established that you will have to dedicate your life to plying a trade in order to achieve greatness. The same can be said if you are to maintain this level for any significant period of time. What we have not discussed is what price does one pay in the pursuit of sustained superiority? We can quickly eliminate anyone not willing to tax themselves mentally and physically along the way.

"I think you're suffering from Post Traumatic Stress Syndrome," the father of five boys told me. 'How could this be?' I asked myself, especially since I was a teacher and not in the military. I did not know civilians could suffer such a fate, and didn't allow myself to seriously entertain this idea at first, out of respect for actual servicemen and women.

But this was the conclusion that the father of five boys came to after hearing me complain of a list of ailments which appeared to be physical in nature. After 25 years in the field of education and not long after my 50th birthday, my health seemed in decline. I had fainting spells and dizziness I noticed while I was at work. Sometimes, I would be in front of a group of kids or talking to a co-worker and felt like I were about to pass out. There were moments I would speak and I couldn't belief the gibberish coming out of my mouth. My words seemed mangled and nonsensical.

I realized it wasn't just me when a colleague asked, "are you okay?" Was I having a stroke? Somehow, magically, when I got in my car and headed home, the symptoms seemed to fade. One day, I was walking down the school's hallway, and I felt the floor and walls moving. On other occasions, out of nowhere, I would be panting and short of breath. Oddly enough, this period coincided with me being in some of the best shape of my adult life since I was working out on a regular basis to, ironically, be as healthy as possible.

In the middle of class one day, I couldn't shake the disequilibrium I was feeling, so I asked my co-teacher to take over. I ran down to the main office. I entered the principal's office where he was having a cabinet meeting. "I don't feel well, I need to leave," I said. Again, I must have looked pretty bad, because I could see the look of concern on the assistant principal's face when she said, "Ok, I hope you feel better."

I was overcome with a sense of panic as I rushed to the emergency room of a local hospital. I was so nervous, I was afraid of crashing into the wall on the freeway en route. Another "are you okay?" was the response as I asked a woman in a booth at the hospital where to park to go into emergency. After being checked out and doctors not being able to locate the cause of my symptoms, I was discharged. The next two months were filled with appointments where I had my heart, head and everything in between checked. Still no answers.

Finally, an eye, ear, nose and throat specialist asked, "have you considered talking to a psychologist?" That's when I thought maybe the father of five boys had the correct diagnosis. It finally dawned on me that I was just about to be laid off by my school district a second time and was headed to my fifth school in the past four years. In addition to employment woes, I was also navigating a perfect storm of financial and personal problems.

It took someone on the outside looking in to notice what was happening. When you are in the midst of going through something you can't always see it because, well, **you're in** it. This is why, as we mentioned earlier, a functioning Man Circle is essential. My conversations with veteran educators over the years, confirmed that the levels of stress and anxiety we encounter can be overwhelming at times. I now had personal experience with why they complained about their "nerves" as the reason these teachers had to take sick days, sick leave, which I eventually did, or simply retire, which I also did years later.

My adversity caused me to reflect on how in my younger years, I could hop out of bed on four or five hours rest, blow right through the work day, and hop up the next day and do it all over again. In my 20's and 30's, I used to dismiss employment studies that regularly cited teaching along with air traffic controllers as the most stressful professions. Now, I could no longer afford to do so! After 25 years, the anxiety of a redundant cycle of teaching, meetings, lesson planning, observations, professional developments and conferences, often with incompetent school leaders, were beginning to take their toll.

I even started to have the Sunday morning blues. This occurs when you realize your weekend is about to end and Monday begins the grind anew. As a man, I had a terrible coping strategy: just push through it! The accumulated impact of years of service is universal among professionals. The former NFL coach said the biggest difference between a younger player in the league and an older one is the recovery time. "In his first couple of years, a guy's body starts feeling better (after a Sunday game) by Tuesday. With a veteran, it may take until Thursday or Friday."

My co-teacher, who was already on a run of more than a decade of exemplary instruction, was once asked about a peer who was in her first few years. The administration hailed the new teacher as the second coming of the Christ because of how well she implemented the current wave of teaching practices in her classroom. "Yeah, but let's see how well she does 10 years from now," my co-teacher said, clearly referring to burnout.

I believe the field of education is a great laboratory for our topic of endurance because it demonstrates how relatively non-physical labor extracts a fatigue which has physical manifestations. In urban school districts, we worked right alongside police officers who had an entirely different perspective in dealing with children. Let's just say many of them were "hands-on." For the most part, I thought this deterrent was definitely needed. I felt a mutual respect when they would say, "I couldn't do what you do."

I took this to mean the officers appreciated the tolerance and patience we showed with children and sometimes, even worse, some of the adults. But it was hard for me to equate "my trauma" with theirs, especially those who had served. In one instance, we had a teacher who was venting about work. One of our school's officers thought her grievances were trivial. Like Mark Johnson, he was a veteran of the United States' campaign in Iraq. The teacher's petty gripes served as a trigger for this normally mild-mannered public school servant. "I saw a partner of mine get his head blown off right next to me, but you don't hear me complaining!"

While unfortunate, the officer's remarks provide an invaluable perspective. Johnson, as a former math teacher and veteran, is uniquely qualified to compare the two fields. What they have in common is, "you always have to be ready." The difference is, in front of a group of students, "you're not thinking about **death.**"

If one were to ever wonder if the physical and mental sacrifices required for honor are worth it, the *The Art of War* gives us a simple test. "What causes opponents to come of their own accord is the prospect of **gain**. What discourages opponents from coming is the prospect of **harm**." Furthermore, "If you reward your men with spoils, that will make them fight of their own initiative, so the enemy's goods can be taken. *That is why it is said that where there are big rewards there are valiant men.*"

Thus, it is for each man to decide whether the "rewards" of his labor justify the price he must pay. An attorney, as in the one above, may risk his life if he has a fervent belief in his case or if the potential settlement is substantial. An educator may not fret about conditions if he's convinced that the intrinsic compensation for making a difference in the lives of a few children is worth it. Athletes are celebrated for placing both life and limb in jeopardy for fame and fortune. For example, players in the NFL compare the contact on each play to being in a car accident.

Detroit Pistons great Isiah Thomas' persistence with a broken leg during a Game Seven loss to the Los Angeles Lakers in the 1988 NBA Finals, set the tone and modeled the resolve required for the team's championships in 1989 and 1990. Players often state that the difference between competing for hardware and winning it is what you're willing to **give up**. When men say that "everyone wants to go to heaven, but no one wants to die," we're talking about "leaving it **all** out there." In college, they call it "giving your body to the university."

The military tells you to "fight for the guy next to you." A football player may be so sore that he may not want to go to practice the next day, but will do so anyway because he doesn't want to let a teammate down. There are also times we learn the sacrifice necessary for glory from a heated rival. In the 1983 National Hockey League Finals, the New York Islanders swept the Edmonton Oilers on their home ice for the Islanders' fourth straight Stanley Cup championship. Edmonton's "Great One" Wayne Gretzky said a "turning point" was an observation the Oilers made after putting on their suits and they began heading out the Nassau Coliseum.

In particular, Gretzky was not excited about the raucous celebration he and his teammates expected to witness once they walked past the Islanders' room where players and family gathered. But to their surprise, the champs, especially the vets, were not in an overly "festive mood." The room had all the ambiance of a "MASH unit." Gretzky described the victors as "battered and bruised" with "ice bags and heat packs all over their body." Although he felt his team were fresh enough to go another round, Gretzky realized they needed to "pay the price" the Islanders had, if they were to **win it all**. The Oilers did, as they won five of the next seven Stanley Cups!

## MAN CODE 4:6 RESPONDING TO CRITICS: ACTIONS SPEAK LOUDER THAN WORDS

But a winner is not only a man who just "does his job" at an elite level. The Man Code sets the bar high because it demands more than accepting the ebbs and flows which naturally go with the territory of being a professional. The Code also places a premium on refusing to wither in the face of sometimes blistering criticism of one's performance, whether it is justified or not! This is simple. Some men are legendary recipients of accolades or kudos for their or the team's performance, but quickly find a desk or bench to slide under when adversity calls.

They will ask "how do I look?" before addressing the public when the occasion is celebratory. However, these same men will renege on the invitation and ask a trusted assistant to field questions or handle the matter when disaster strikes. Several such "leaders" were addressed in Chapter Three. We will continue to affirm that leadership is a verb not a noun, and bearing the title does not necessarily mean you fit the description. I always respected those who would take responsibility for their charges publicly, and correct you in private if it were your mistake. Generally, subordinates are more loyal to this brand of supervision and work harder as a result.

Athletes and entertainers perform in the public eye and are critiqued publicly too. Jack Nicholas had a poor performance in a tournament once. Afterwards, several reporters marveled at how patient he was answering questions about his less than stellar outing. Few professions exist that are shielded from some form of public disapprobation. In education, teachers and leaders must always be wary of someone "waiting outside" if they feel they have been victimized by an unfavorable disposition regarding academics or discipline.

Children sometimes prey on a teacher's fear by making statements like, "You don't want to call my mother, because she'll cuss you out!" to dissuade you from communicating an issue or problem. For the most part, these kids are exaggerating. But regardless, I would laugh and say, "If your mother curses me out, that's alright. I'm still getting paid. I'll just document it since that's part of the job **too**." I would remind the children that "there a lot of things you put up with at work that you would never put up with in your personal life."

A common refrain uttered by hostile parents and community members when school leaders make a tough call concerning their children or loved ones is, "I'm going to your supervisor!" Those who actually have the stomach for the position will reply undeterred, "Here, let me give you their number!" Message sent! There are times, however, when the problem comes from inside not outside of the building. I was complaining about my peers one day when a colleague provided me with some timeless wisdom. "Just be happy you don't have to take them home with you."

We mentioned the instances of our attorney receiving death threats. Well, imagine judges, many of whom live among the service community. There will be unpopular decisions and citizens who are without scruples in reminding these public figures. Frank Serpico, a famous New York police officer known for exposing corruption within the department in the 1960's and 70's, said his father taught him a lesson that stuck. "Never run when you're right!" Of course, this is easier said than done.

Because any man knows that iron sharpens iron, we must respectfully receive constructive appraisals of our work. However, we must always consider the source. If the detractors own a proven track record of having our best interests at heart, so much the better. The litmus test is are they correct?

If a planner wanted to manage your money, wouldn't you first vet their success rate with other clients, or better yet, inquire how well they have invested their **own**? Why wouldn't we hold "the experts," especially those who haven't established themselves in the field, to the same standard?

Many times, criticism is jealousy in disguise. Or is it your fault that you have been created by a force of nature to perform as you have and others wish they were you? In this era of the proliferation of social media, we tend to forget one simple fact; If we spend more time thinking about and responding to arm chair analysts than we do honing our craft, maybe it's time we take a seat next to them. Often, critics can be similar to our topic in Chapter One: bullies. Comedian Chris Rock said that if someone is not feeding you and can't whip you, you don't have to listen to them! Since Rock was really discussing children, this advice would be even more applicable to grown men.

The decisions made by even select practitioners in the professional world, bear life or death consequences, and the ability to "face the music" when things "go left" distinguish the weak from the strong. An old adage is that lawyers send their mistakes to prison and doctors send theirs to the morgue. Everyone is familiar with the expression tough times don't last, but tough people do. When faced with contrary fate, the circumstances force us to examine why we chose our respective lines of work and whether it is still worth it.

## MAN CODE 4:7 KNOW WHEN TO SAY WHEN

In "Chapter Four: Coming Early and Staying Late," the road map to fulfilling our destinies is a mountain we must scale, and each section of this chapter serves as a base. Before we begin our ascent, a vision manifests itself. From there, we put in the work necessary to actualize the plan. Opportunities will present themselves along the way, and it is imperative that we take advantage of them before they vanish into thin air. Since we have trained long and hard for the moment at hand, it is difficult to contain our excitement!

But we must trust in our preparation and let faith guide the journey. Next, the higher we climb, the greater the altitude and the less the margin of error since each step is critical to our mission. The entire operation requires sacrifice, so therefore, we must monitor the influence of detractors if we are about elevation and not idle conversation.

If you have enjoyed longevity while sustaining a commitment to greatness in your calling, then you have followed the instructions. After you have conquered the mountain repeatedly and viewed it from its peak while blazing a path for others, there is only one question. How long will you continue? Your die-hard warrior spirit has brought you to this juncture, but it can also be your undoing.

Tzu has some thoughts on the matter. "When you do battle, even if you are winning, if you continue for a long time it will dull your forces and blunt your edge..." In other words, Tzu is saying we should not stay at the party too long. At this stage, a combatant is in august company; gray hair and gray skies are indicative of a change. Far from the spring of our campaign, the onward march of time signals that we have reached the winter of our engagement. Or as a coach once told me, "We're on the back nine."

The decision to retire from a career of service should not be taken lightly, but must be confronted nonetheless. There is a time and a season for everything, and you and only you know when that is. In education, that time is when you start to say, 'I keep getting older, but the students stay the same age.'

Detroit Lions Hall of Fame running back Barry Sanders made the process sound simple. When Sanders announced he was shutting it down, none of his trademark evasiveness was put on display. In fact, Sanders was very direct. The iconic athlete said his desire not to play was greater than his desire to play. Let this be our standard!

It is well known that men have a responsibility to protect, provide, and proclaim. This chapter started with a proclamation and described a process that will allow us to provide. In the next chapter, we will address how we plan to protect ourselves and loved ones as we discuss security.

# CHAPTER FIVE:

## *Security: To Be Forewarned Is To Be Forearmed*

**No discussion of Man** principles would be complete without an examination of protection protocols. You have made it to this point, in life as well as in the essay, because you have already applied some of this information. During the analysis, actual engagement will be a last resort. If you have an appetite for gratuitous violence, I suggest you find a violent video game. Since the objective is to salvage our lives and limbs and those of others, the methods used must serve this end.

As men, there will be those looking to us to make correct assessments. The approach is basic: detection, avoidance, and if all else fails, whatever is necessary to defend ourselves and loved ones. To keep the emphasis on survival and not the glorification of mayhem, each non-fiction illustration is a cautionary tale. Some will involve young men to contrast the folly of youth with the more calculated responses of mature males.

In the Chapter One examination of bullying, we identified restless aggression as a natural and necessary aspect of healthy male functioning, particularly if is channeled correctly. But as adults, we are cognizant of the pitfalls of selling wolf tickets and incessantly tugging on Superman's cape!

Before we begin, I would invite anyone so inclined to train with an expert like Kevin in Chapter One in the use of their hands, and/or a marksman in the use of arms, to prepare for situations where you are left with no other recourse. If you've met "Bus Stop," also in Chapter One, you know that your mouth can get you in trouble that it can't get you out of. We'll start by scanning the environment.

## MAN CODE 5:1 THE FIRST LAW OF SELF-DEFENSE IS SELF-AWARENESS

A man's competence in assessing threats in the immediate surroundings is a combination of genetics and training. The two merge when his protective hardware and skills acquired over time become one. Sometimes, we can **sense** trouble is on the horizon. In addition, we are taught to size up situations and people. Fundamentals such as keep your eyes on the door wherever we find ourselves, come to mind.

But no matter how much knowledge we have, we should never disregard our sixth sense. One summer after Stan and I had graduated, I went South to spend part of my vacation at my grandparents' house. One night, Stan and I went out to a club on the city's Eastside. A young lady whom Stan knew had caught my attention. We were leaving when I decided to continue talking to her outside the front door.

Gradually, a crowd began to amass near the street and, even though the group wasn't loud, it generated an eerie buzz that made me uncomfortable. I sped up my conversation and got her number. "Stan, let's go," I said. The next morning, I read the Sunday edition of the local newspaper that was placed each day on the front porch. I noted a story about a fatal shooting on the Eastside Saturday night. It was where Stan and I were. I checked the time. The shooting was about 15 minutes after we left and a few feet from where I was standing. The next day, I called Stan to tell him. What I told myself was I would always trust my instincts.

Previously, Tzu stated that we must "win" before going into "battle." This means doing our prep. Opportunities to detect, deflect, and de-escalate are determined upon entry. This is true regardless of location, be it our homes, classrooms, or businesses and other establishments. Toxic energy must be duly noted and dealt with. In my classroom, I would stand at the door and greet every student before he or she walked in. Those who wouldn't speak or displayed disrespectful or negative body language would have to stand off to the side. I would briefly confer with them. They may not make it in the room if I am not satisfied with their explanation. Why should one or two children be allowed to compromise the learning environment for the entire class?

However, a man entrusted with the responsibilities of protection, can only do better if he knows better. Best practices for event security are to speak to all and note their feedback and body language. Those who don't speak, grunt, or appear agitated or upset become the focal point. Keep an eye on them until they exit!

Although congeniality is rarely part of the playbook in the training of security personnel, it needs to be! A warm greeting can go a long way in making patrons comfortable and defusing any tension they may bring to the venue. Standing around flexing muscles and "mean mugging" those whom enter, create a negative aura which sometimes makes your job harder because such demeanor invites confrontation.

The owner of a personal security firm provides us with further insights. His clientele is professional athletes, celebrities, entertainers, and their families. The security team this gentleman assembled is comprised of mostly former law enforcement officers spread across the United States who are licensed to carry firearms. Of course, the weapons are to be used judiciously.

A typical assignment would be for a celebrity to request a presence for an out of town trip which might include visits to nightclubs and restaurants. But the members of this group are not flying by the seats of their pants, there is a process they follow. Typically, security would call ahead to the destination, speak to management, identify himself and the client, and inform them when they planned on arriving.

Once security shows up with the man or woman of the hour, they introduce themselves. Next, there's agreement on a seating arrangement with the business' staff so the guests can be quickly located in the event of any problems. This is a significant step to ensure that the personal security is on the same page as the venue's. The men employed at this firm have a simple strategy: if a potential situation arises, escort the client out of the establishment as expeditiously as possible to avoid a costly confrontation. It is not uncommon for people who have nothing to lose, to instigate an incident with the rich and famous in the hopes of suing.

The firm's worst clients, according to the owner, were players in the National Football League. Why? Because if an altercation broke out, instead of following the lead of security and exiting immediately, the players wanted to handle it themselves. The liability was not worth it. Hence, the agency stopped providing services for these professional athletes.

Despite the above, the same strength and aggression that can be a liability, will cause businesses, especially ones that sell alcohol, to employ former football players as security. What we must remember, however, is that customers should always be treated with dignity, and those who are inebriated, are not necessarily easier to reason with or remove. Sometimes, being intoxicated may mean that a man may, in the moment, be immune to pain and seem to possess super human strength. They should still be given the same options as everyone else.

Dave, a former collegiate offensive lineman who did bar security, had two questions for those who were disorderly. On approach, the offender or offending party would be asked, "Is there a problem?" If the miscreant did not provide an acceptable answer, the query that would follow would force him to consider if his affairs were in order. Dave's next question? "Is **this** what you want?"

## MAN CODE 5:2 NEVER TURN YOUR BACK ON AN ADVERSARY

Nearly 20 years ago, I had a witty junior named Darwin Smith in my high school English class. He was bright and disarming and never lacked confidence. In fact, Mr. Smith was a little cocky. Darwin wasn't experiencing the same struggles as many of his classmates since his mother had a good job in corporate America. Although I always invited his participation in class discussions, sometimes

I had to share what was not a well-kept secret. "Darwin, you talk too much."

Sure enough, Darwin was standing with other students at the stop one day while waiting for the bus that would take him back home. Out of nowhere a man yelled, "I'll give anyone $50 dollars if they sock this mother#$%! right here!" while pointing to another man in the crowd. Everyone was silent except for Darwin. "I'll do it!!" he boasted. However, Darwin did not *do* it.

Darwin and the rest of the group then boarded the bus. After getting off, Darwin took the short walk to his block and was about to make the turn on his street. Apparently, Darwin forgot what he promised before he hopped on the bus. But the would-be victim didn't. The man rushed Darwin and made a formal introduction by planting his fist on Darwin's jaw. Mr. Smith had to have his jaw wired.

After missing a few days, Darwin returned to class. As his teacher, I decided to do something unusual. Because Mr. Smith was so talkative and not easily embarrassed, I had him recount his side of the story. I wanted the entire class in on the lesson. Darwin finished his version with, "But he sucker punched me, Mr. Woods!" "Darwin, what did I always tell you?" "I talk too much," he said, his head slightly bowed and his voice a few decibels lower.

Furthermore, I called attention to the fact that Darwin turned his back on an adversary that he created and an attack he provoked. This was a teachable moment because Darwin was reminded that he was lucky since the assault could have been worse and his jaw would eventually heal. He also should have been motivated not to repeat this mistake. For those wondering what Darwin's encounter has to do with school, my answer would be it doesn't, unless you're also teaching **survival**.

## MAN CODE 5:3 NEVER JUDGE A BOOK BY ITS COVER

In my next assignment, I was at a rough-and-tumble high school on the Westside. But many of the staff, particularly the administrators, seemed up to the challenge. Previously, we mentioned that every occupation has its shortcomings and mastering them is key. At this high school, a number of staff, including myself, found that defending ourselves and pressing assault charges against students in the aftermath, were occupational hazards.

A noteworthy episode involved our athletic director who was also an assistant principal. At 5' 7", Bill, who is now a high school principal, was unremarkable physically, with the possible exception of how vascular he was, particularly his arms and forearms. There were other details that many of us adults were privy to, that the children weren't. They might have witnessed Bill's ill-tempered nature at times, but had no clue what lie beneath it. He was known for taking on all comers. The kids also probably weren't aware of how hyper-competitive Bill was or of his proficiency in the martial arts.

But that was about to change. While the educator was attempting to clear a second floor hallway notoriously crowded with truant students, a young man decided it was his lucky day. Bill asked the student, who was 6'3", several times to go to class. However, he ignored him and called the man everything but a child of God.

Finally, this young man swung at the administrator. In short order, the kid was face down on the floor. What happened? Bill leg whipped him, chopping the young man down to size. The ensuing gathering of insolent children, who, at first, were cheering for this boy, begged Bill to show him some mercy. He did. Instead of following his instincts, and striking a debilitating blow to the back of the kid's neck, Bill held him long enough for the public safety officers to arrest him.

Later, in court, the student's mother was stunned to find out she could be sued for damages. The mistake this kid made was obvious. He thought he was going to overpower the administrator because of his eight-inch height advantage. What he didn't realize was though he was big, he was still a **boy**, and made a mistake that could have cost him more than a bruised ego. The young man learned the first lesson of manhood: **repercussions and consequences.**

But all children are not created equal. There are those who simply do not partake in idle chatter. I met a few of these students as a substitute teacher at a high school on the Southwest side of the city. Sometimes a fellow staff member, generally a counselor, would come to my classroom door with a bombshell. "Woods, that kid is in a gang," they would tell me while discretely identifying a boy sitting quietly at his desk. "That one right there?" I would ask with a puzzled look on my face.

What I discovered was these young men were **not** as innocent as they **appeared**. They were members of local gangs who were connected to an international crime syndicate. The boys displayed a different side in the streets where anything goes. Many times, the rare occasion they would attend school, was when it was "too hot" out there for them: getting written up and being kicked out would defeat the purpose. There was nothing or no one in the school house they were afraid of since these young men had jumped out of the sand box and broken across the line separating the kids from the adults' side of the playground a long time ago. Their demeanor gave credence to the notion that **"it's the quiet ones you've got to watch."**

Ohio State running back Archie Griffin became the only player in college football history to win two Heisman Trophies when he repeated in 1975. Shortly thereafter, the diminutive star, who was generously listed at 5'9", inspired a catchphrase which is still a mantra for the underdogs of today: "It's not the size of the dog in the fight, it's the size of the **fight** in the dog."

*The Art of War* discourages gauging our foes based on the superficial because, "A military operation involves deception. Even though you are competent, appear to be incompetent. Though effective, appear to be ineffective."

The aforementioned stories bring us to another great lesson that can be related to engagement, temperament, which is a function of readiness. This means bringing the intensity and resolve to the **moment** in question in order to prevail. Coach Wooden called this, "being at your best **when** your best is required." In addition, all of the firepower or arm talent in the world mean nothing if they cannot be harnessed at the appropriate time. Having a weapon at your disposal and being prepared to use it may be two different matters.

## MAN CODE 5:4 RESPECT ALL, FEAR NONE

When Bill left to accept a position at another school, the void was instantly filled by the Hulk-like presence of Tracy, who also held the dual roles of assistant principal and athletic director. Sometimes appearances can deceive, as in the above case of unassuming students who were gang-affiliated. In other instances, first impressions can be deadly accurate. If you saw the 6' 4" 270+ pound Tracy and your initial impression was of a bruiser, you would be quite correct. His head and neck could easily take up a parking space. He was a former collegiate football player who had extensive training as a boxer and martial artist.

Moreover, Tracy's exploits were not confined to a ring or formal setting. In the streets, the big man was legendary for assisting anyone get acquainted with the emergency room of their local hospital. I once had a problem with something Tracy said, so following the Code, I brought it to his attention man to man. However, knowing his background, I made sure I expressed myself in a calm tone of voice while giving him some space. I did not know what Tracy would say, but when he apologized, that told me that when you brought him respect, you would be received with respect.

Somehow, not all of the students got this! As in the incident with Bill, on one occasion, Tracy was clearing the hall after the bell rang, this time near the gymnasium, when a young man who was defying a request to go to class or identify himself, became belligerent. Although I was headed upstairs to my office, I couldn't believe what I was witnessing, so I stood there to see how this would all play out.

The situation escalated quickly. The student, who was about 6'2" but so skinny he'd have to jump around in the shower to get wet, told Tracy "F--- you. I will f---- you up!" repeatedly. I started wondering what planet was this child on? Even if Tracy weren't who he was, and were a perfect prophet of non-violence who passed out flowers at the airport, why chance it and defy such an imposing authority figure? When I examined the young man more closely, I think I had my answer. 'Oh, my God,' I thought, 'he's high!!' The kids' lids were so closed, you would have needed a forklift to open them.

My next thought was, 'This young man just wasted his drug money, because his buzz is about to be killed.' "What did you say you're going to do to me? What did you say you're going to do to me, mother#*****!!!" Tracy replied. Frame One: The kid punched away and it looked almost comical because his arms only extended sideways instead of at their intended target. This was because Tracy's hand made a beeline for the boy's sternum as his ginormous paw became a fist while locking onto the young man's shirt (Tracy's hand looked like it engulfed the entirety of the boy's chest). Frame Two: He pressed the student into the wall behind him. Frame Three: With the same hand, Tracy pulled the young man by his shirt off the wall and slammed him on the floor.

Needless to say, the intervention ended the hissy fit the boy was having. Several days later, a man in his 30's or 40's who was 6' built like a tank and had a Carhartt jacket on, entered the back door and marched down the hallway near where the incident occurred. "I need to talk to the man who put the scratch on my son's head," he said. "He is not here right now," I stated. Eventually, the educator and the boy's father had a conference.

Tracy would have been justified in laying all the blame at the child's feet, but he didn't. He took some of the responsibility. "Dad, me and your son f----d up," Tracy said. The father displayed more sense than his son by accepting Tracy's apology. But the school's AP wasn't conciliatory because he was scared of the boy or his father. Tracy was merely practicing diplomacy.

The knowledge that you have already won allows you to negotiate from a position of strength. This is what Tzu means when he states the objective of war is to "change the heart of your enemy." In doing so, it is necessary to draw the line between the use of reasonable and excessive force. Discretion is always advised when engagement is warranted, otherwise, the strategy could easily backfire.

Anthony, a vice president of a community college, has direct experience in why there is a downside to the use of heavy-handed approaches in dealing with grown men. Late one night, Anthony ventured out to one of his favorite clubs. He entered, took a seat, and got comfortable. Soon, a man who appeared to be in a jovial mood, sat next to him. The man offered to buy Anthony a drink. Because he didn't know the gentleman, or his intentions, he initially declined. The stranger insisted. Finally, Anthony said, "Okay, but the next one is on me."

After turning up his drink a few times, the man felt relaxed enough to strike up a conversation with a woman there. But apparently, he made a request that she was not interested in honoring. In return, the man called her the magic word. The woman signaled to the club's security. When the bouncers arrived, they told him he had to leave. However, if that weren't enough, to ensure they delivered their message loud and clear, security made sure they roughed up the man before throwing him out.

Anthony totally disagreed with the staff's interaction with this patron. "They didn't have to do **that**." He was convinced that despite, or perhaps because of the man's inappropriate language, a more corporate stance was in order. Basically, Anthony didn't think this was the time or place to get into a pissing contest with a skunk! "I would have told him, look man, you've had too much to drink, we're going to have to ask you to leave (which gives him an **option**). But the next time you come back, the drinks are on us." Instead, the swift series of rejections by the woman and then the security team, shattered the gentleman's dignity.

The stranger went to his car and quickly returned. He pushed past the security at the door, pulled out a gun and showered the club with a hail of bullets. This vengeful attack left one of the bouncers dead and several staff and customers critically injured. Where was Anthony during all the commotion? "I was under the table."

The next day, this incident was prominently reported on the television news. "I was there," he remembered telling his wife.

As we learn to respect others, we must not abuse the respect that we are accorded. A retreat is not necessarily an act of cowardice. An animal is most dangerous when it is cornered. Human beings are no exception. "Do not press a desperate enemy," Tzu writes. The Code also suggests that we heed the words of a man who served as private security for the figurehead of one the most ruthless recording companies in history. His time in supermax facilities only sharpened his thinking on the matter. "If I am running from you, do not chase after me!"

## MAN CODE 5:5 DON'T BE A HERO WHILE TRYING TO IMPRESS A WOMAN

A man had not been out in a while so one night, he decided to head to an establishment which was an old standby. He parked his car not far away. As he attempted to cross the intersection near the front door, the man noticed a well-worn van heading in his direction. He stopped and so did the van. When he proceeded, the van moved forward also. Apparently, the pedestrian and the woman behind the wheel just got their wires crossed. But the passenger, a male, didn't see it that way. "What is wrong with you?" the passenger yelled, but actually, in not such nice terms. The pedestrian shouted something just as profane and disrespectful back.

At first, the pedestrian almost went back to his car and drove home. He merely wanted to have a good time, not get into an altercation over something childish. But he figured, 'No, I'm out now. I **am** going in and I'll leave when **I** am ready." Meanwhile, the instigator jumped out of the passenger door and went right past the security at the entrance without paying. The man took note of this as well as the fact that the passenger couldn't have been that smart to have entered in front of him with his back turned (Man Code 5:2).

The pedestrian saw the man go all the way to the rear and through the saloon-style doors leading to the kitchen area. Evidently, the hot head was an employee. The pedestrian then recognized Otis, a friend who was also a counselor, sitting at the bar, and decided to take a seat next to him. The man's purpose for sitting there was two-fold: 1) The pedestrian could blow off some steam while enjoying the company of a partner 2) He was near a collection of large bottles, in the event he had to defend himself.

While the man was relating the incident to Otis, he told Otis he was watching his back just in case the aggressor resurfaced. Otis, who specializes in counseling incarcerated males, gave the man a different perspective. The therapist said the confrontation sounded like a classic case of a guy trying to act tough in order to impress a lady friend. "Chill man, don't say anything (if the guy were to return). At least half the cats locked up are in jail over a **woman**." The pedestrian felt it was providential that he had such wisdom in his Man Circle.

A second kind of difficulty that can put a man in conflict with respect to his female companion, particularly in public settings, is how she is dressed. The more revealing she makes herself, the more attention will likely be showered upon her, and the greater the likelihood that some of it will be negative. Every time a woman decides what to wear, she could be potentially taking her man's life into her own hands.

But this is a matter of personal preference as some gentlemen feel flattered that their lady is recognized. Others, including yours truly, will settle for modesty because it brings about less security issues. We have already covered what the Code says about making moves on a woman we know is with someone else, so that does not bear repeating.

The Egyptian high priest Ptahhotep, in his *The Oldest Book in the World* (circa 2480 BCE), has some advice. "If you want friendship to endure in the house that you enter, the house of a master, of a brother or of a friend, then whatever place you enter beware of approaching the women there" (Verse 18). Further Ptahhotep notes, "Unwelcome is he who intrudes on them." To this we can add, even if the female is the romantic interest of a friend, out of respect, always address your partner first. We are sure you would want this same courtesy extended to you.

## MAN CODE 5:6 IF YOU'RE NOT IN IT, YOU SHOULDN'T BE AROUND IT

In the introduction, it was stated that you may debate the validity of ideas such as Code 5:6 at your own peril. But just because I disagree that gravity exists, doesn't mean I will survive a plunge from a 10-story building. As elders, we have innumerable corollaries for Code 5:6, such as be where you are supposed to be when you are supposed to be there, and do what you are supposed to do when you are supposed to do it. Perhaps the most disturbing consequence of not adhering to this order is "bullets have no names."

A few years ago, I had an upperclassmen, a young man whom, despite not being a Rhodes scholar, I took an interest in because of his natural leadership abilities. He always seemed to say the right thing and be an encouragement to his classmates and me. However, I detected an erratic attendance pattern, so I decided to approach him about it one day after class. He said he had to work late at night and was so tired, he couldn't make it to school.

But this congenial kid was not employed at McDonald's, Burger King, or Kentucky Fried Chicken, like many of his peers. He told me almost as a matter of fact, that he worked in a dope house. "I'm tired of seeing my mother struggle to pay the light bill." These conversations raise all kind of ethical issues for educators because they deal with child welfare and may point to endangerment and neglect. On the other hand, when the youth is 17, how effective are the school's resource staff going to be in providing this kind of student with a realistic alternative?

In these situations, I tried my best not to sound like former First Lady Nancy Reagan by telling children, 'Just say no to drugs.' Even though I knew I didn't have a job lined up for him, I went ahead and explained the obvious, that I understood how dire his circumstances were, but I didn't think this line of work was worth the risks.

One day when class was over, the young man came up to me with what looked to be a sigh of relief. "Mr. Woods, I don't work there any longer. The house was shot up!" Fortunately, he wasn't there when the attack occurred. "I'm just glad **you're** alright," I said. Not knowing or wanting to know the details of the incident, I slept better that night because I was relieved too.

Our second and final case, however, does not have a happy ending. In fact, the tragedy of errors committed by the main character, resulted in him being a footnote in the career of a hit man who was the subject of an episode of *America's Most Evil*. In my first work experience outside of the classroom, I found myself in a Curriculum

Coordinator position at an alternative high school. Basically, I was the number two in command after the principal.

An instance that stood out was when the principal asked me to check to see if a teacher were in his room during a period class was scheduled. When I went to Brian's room, he was not there and neither were the students. To his credit, he had a small group of only about five kids. He probably just left them with another teacher and went somewhere, I thought. I went back down to the main office to inform the principal that Brian was nowhere in sight.

Apparently because this had happened before, the principal told me to write the teacher up for transgressions of work rules related to insubordination, since Brian was not with his class and did not get permission to go elsewhere. Negligence was implied since the instructor was not physically able to verify the whereabouts of his students. I did not know Brian well, so I had not formed much an opinion of him, other than to wonder if he went swimming every morning or had allergies: his pupils always seemed to be dilated. Of course, I made a mental note of Brian's somnambulance since I was supervising him.

At this point, the knowledge of whether someone is inebriated is not necessarily a breach of the Man Code. What an adult does on their time is their business. Moreover, there is a time and a place for everything. But as it relates to work, generally speaking, being sober on the job is not a bad idea. Exceptions may include wine makers or taste testers. If your career of choice calls for you to judge the quality of what's in the barrel, your day at work will be much different than a pilot of a major airline. However, if "you always have to be ready," as Mark Johnson suggests, there is no reason for not having all of your faculties together, especially in a school setting, where you may be compromising child safety. Beyond that, what kind of conduct is an adult modeling for children, when he can't even wait to punch the clock before he starts unwinding?

After I printed a copy of Brian's disciplinary letter, I took it to his room. By this time, he was back at his desk. Instead of putting the correspondence in Brian's box, I handed it to him to ensure he got it. I then left to return to the main office. Unbeknownst to me, Brian was not far behind. Even though he was not directly in my rear, I felt I should have noticed him. By the time I did, I looked up and Brian had slammed the taped write up on a supply cabinet in the main office for all to see. "You can keep this, HOME BOY!" he barked impudently.

In my more than two decades plus of service to the district, I had not witnessed such a raw display of rebelliousness from an **adult.** Brian's creativity was astounding. He adhered a warning notice from a supervisor and prominently posted it in the main office, of all places. Why hadn't I thought of doing something like that? Right, now I know, probably because I planned on keeping my job.

When I reported the young educator's bizarre behavior to the principal, he insisted that a second disciplinary letter should follow. Because I documented Brian's comments as well as his obstinate tone, this time, he was being charged with a threat to staff. Brian was released from his teaching assignment. The last time I saw him was a few months later. Brian was in the school's gym one day talking to another teacher. He was probably trying to garner some sympathy in the wake of his termination. Even though Brian wasn't supposed to be on the grounds of any district school, particularly this one, I decided against having him forcibly removed from the premises. 'Let him have his moment,' I thought.

Obviously, it was a huge ask for Brian to comply with even the most basic rules of the workplace. But now that he was liberated from the oppressive restrictions that gainful employment placed on him, we will examine how well he fared in conforming to the rules of the streets. We already demonstrated that everybody wants to be a gangster until the real ones show up on the scene. In similar fashion, it seems everyone thinks they're a gorilla, until they end up in the forest.

More than a year would pass before we would hear of Brian again. I was in a new assignment. Oddly enough, there were staff in this building who knew him from the previous school. Another interesting turn to the tale was there were also instructors here who taught the man who would eventually take his life. One, a notoriously tough grader, was a senior English teacher in my department who was a 40-year veteran. So it came as somewhat of a surprise when this educator, who rarely doled out compliments, described her former student as highly intelligent. She also added that he was "a good looking guy, the girls were crazy about him."

But the young man's love of life and learning was snuffed out when a stray bullet killed his younger sister. From there, a pall fell over him and a gloominess pervaded his countenance. In fact, he missed his graduation because he was locked up for stealing a car. Although he was a skilled tradesman, the young man's life took a dramatic about-face once he discovered how lucrative a career in "waste management" could be. Jobs where he could rid the world of dope men, like the one who took his sister's life, were like icing on the cake, because they allowed him to extract a measure of revenge.

Let's clear the air about a common misconception. There are those who question the intellect of individuals who choose the criminal lifestyle. They are drawn to a life of crime because they can't make it in educational settings or any segment of society that requires a strong mind, according to this school of thought. The former 40-year educator would quickly dismiss this notion. "He wasn't the first of my honor students who turned to murder for hire," she said in an interview with the *New Yorker* magazine.

"It was a mental exercise for him, for sure," according to one man familiar with the killer, "the homework, the plotting. The deed of the murder itself." The executioner confirmed his level of preparation for a "job." "My standard practice before a hit was to observe my targets and study their habits for weeks in advance, so I could better plan my strategy for murder," he said in an affidavit. "I am a very careful planner, and I always did everything I could to prevent anything going wrong during a hit."

Although a slaying involving a local public official would follow that would get plenty of press, the incident that gained the killer international acclaim occurred in an urban killing field in a neighborhood known as "The Red Zone." As with much of his other work, the subject was a drug dealer. The young man received the name, address, aliases, and car or cars the victim would be driving. In addition, as is usual and customary, more than a month went into the master plan.

The stake outs included playing baseball in the street with a friend near the subject's house, and sitting in his vehicle, which had tinted windows, watching and observing. One night, a neighbor who normally sits on the porch across the street wasn't outside. This seemed like the perfect time to check how secure the dope man's house was. "I wanted to determine whether (he) left the storm door unlocked, or whether I needed to bring tools to break in."

The hit man was accompanied by a trusted associate in the event things went awry. As they approached the house, they noticed the occupants were cheering loudly. A game was on. This is perfect, the young man thought, because he wouldn't be heard checking the security door. There was a silhouette of a man standing near the side window, and the associate was asked to keep his assault weapon pointed at him in case anything jumped off. Unfortunately, the hit man said, as he reached for the handle on the screen, **the entry door flung open! A man who turned out to be Brian was now face to face with the killer!**

We were told that Brian and his girlfriend planned to relocate to the West Coast in the coming days. But the couple would never make it!

Brian quickly pivoted, an indication he had seen the shooter. There was no turning back now. The reconnaissance exercise had turned into the actual mission. Of course Brian was first. By the time the fusillade of gunfire was complete, four people were slain. The list included the target, Brian's girlfriend, who was a friend of the dealer, and the man who cast the shadow in the window. On the way out, the hit man and his partner exchanged fire with the neighbor, who emerged from inside his home after hearing the ruckus. In an ironic twist, the neighbor, a police chaplain, was a relative of the dope man.

Thus ended the saga of Brian. It was reported that the assault left him so disfigured, he had a closed casket at his funeral. But for the assassin, who is serving several life sentences, this assignment was merely an interlude—his career continued and the body count would reach the teens before he would eventually be nabbed and found guilty.

You may ponder why a tale of woe such as this merited an extended treatment in our section on self-defense. In this chapter, we began with self-knowledge and self-awareness and concluded with a killing spree. Why? Because if Brian, the main character in our last vignette, had more of the former, the latter could have possibly been avoided. Lest we forget, a series of missteps led us to this point!

Although the story had a tragic ending, what did you expect? Some of the most basic tenets of the Man Code relating to self-defense were violated here. Safety is a function of time and place, so it is imperative that we must always be prescient about where we are and our purpose for being there. **There will be a code wherever we find ourselves!**

For some, like Brian's executioner, who was a high achiever academically but grew up around wolves, the street chooses them. But Brian, who lived in the suburbs and whose mother was a high ranking official in the school district, and had other options readily available, **chose the streets.** In fact, we heard Brian's mother was embarrassed by his dismissal.

Some key events foreshadow the young man's demise. First, he showed up to his place of employment under the influence, while flaunting the work rules and recklessly disregarding any semblance of professional decorum and comportment. By doing so, he jeopardized his career and the well-being of the students under his supervision. Next, after being dismissed, Brian had the unmitigated gall to return to the scene of the crime and trespass on school grounds.

It was clear that nobody was going to tell Brian what to do! How do you deal with such unrealistic demands of the workplace like being where you are assigned? Just leave. By literally walking off the job, Brian was now free to roam the streets. With plenty of time on his hands, there was no need to buy some drugs and leave the dope house. He could relax, kick back, prop his feet up and watch the game with his girlfriend, who led him there in the first place.

Early in the chapter, we mentioned that men must always be at the ready because others depend on us to make the right call when it comes to security assessments. Apparently, this young man outsourced such a huge responsibility to his girlfriend. The proof is in the pudding. He couldn't have said, 'honey, I think this is a bad idea,' because he was there too. Other security breaches included, obviously, not being armed in the home of a drug dealer. At least, the target had a gun; his was on the coffee table. But he was too busy eating bullets to reach it.

Moreover, in the chapter's opening, we addressed the importance of watching the door. Of course, that also means **not standing in doorways, which Brian was guilty of, or near windows, which the other young man was doing.** Doors and windows are not just points of entry for people, but bullets as well! It is still not clear why he would unlock the door of *someone else's home*, especially that of a known drug dealer. If you recall, the killer and his wing man only intended to do a security check, the actual deed was slated for another date and time. However, Brian altered this arrangement by literally opening the door of opportunity for the carnage that ensued.

Sometimes we tend to forget that everything in the universe is connected. For every action, there is an equal and opposite reaction. Again, the Code states that just because we can do something, doesn't mean we should. Thus, a man has to be disciplined enough to govern himself accordingly, and must refrain from behaviors that, while gratifying in the short term (3:2), will bring about pain and suffering in the long run. The karma debt built up is like a boomerang which, one day, will revisit its owner. Brian's failure to recognize that if he weren't in it, he shouldn't have been around it, led to the sequence of events which placed him on a collision course with a cold-blooded contract killer.

Finally, I would like to reiterate, this essay is not a horror story. The narrative is not art appreciation or just art for art's sake. If the lessons from this account spare the life of just one young man, they will have served their purpose, and been well worth the time and effort it took to produce them. To write otherwise would violate the letter and spirit of **Code instruction.**

This portion of the paper focused on principles for protecting ourselves and those whom are in our care. The first line of self-defense is self-knowledge and self-awareness. Just as computers use programs to scan them for threats to the hardware, by the same token, we must scan our surroundings for threats as well. We are informed by the objective nature of the environment. But the process is spiritual too, since we must also rely on intuition. Best practices for drawing up any battle plan are to never judge a book by its cover, and to show respect to all while fearing none.

Our effectiveness in keeping ourselves and our women safe is heavily reliant upon how they present and comport themselves. As a famous comedian once said, "You may not be a h___, but you're wearing a h___'s uniform." In addition, monitor any and all energy you might exhibit for the purposes of impressing your lady friend. Don't turn a display of false bravado into your final act!

Again, self-knowledge is critical to the determination of where we are supposed to be and what we are supposed to be doing while there. Fate is like a bear. We are poking it every time we fail to realize that if we are not in something, we shouldn't be **around** it.

Next, I'd like to use the epilogue for reflections and to pay some respects.

# EPILOGUE

When senior point guard Mark Johnson walked off the court after winning the Michigan Class D State Championship in basketball for Detroit East Catholic High School in 1983, he didn't know how he would feel. Was **that** it? 'What's next?' he thought.

Near the end of the 10th and final episode of ESPN's *The Last Chance* documentary, there was a scene which was **not entirely** focused on Michael Jordan's singular brilliance and dominance with the Chicago Bulls of the 1990's. Inspired by a Native American ritual, Hall of Fame Coach Phil Jackson had the team write on a sheet of paper what being part of the 1998 squad that had just won the franchise's sixth championship in eight years, meant to each player. Next, each man shared his reflections with the team.

Jackson then placed their comments along with his in a coffee can and burned them. The significance was this would be the end of the run because the coach and many of the players' contracts weren't being renewed. Coach Wooden could relate to both gentlemen. One of Wooden's favorite quotes was by Cervantes. "The **journey** is better than the inn."

So it is with mixed emotions that I bring this essay to a close. I feel as if I am holding the last page of a family photo album, and together we've been viewing the pictures and images it has captured. Even though we know that every ending is a beginning and every beginning is an ending, a few remarks are in order before we turn the page.

I'd like to start by acknowledging the purpose for this piece. As mentioned in the introduction, I was writing in response to a request that the information be chronicled. Indeed, it has been my pleasure because, as you already know, I am merely a vessel of the greater good. I am neither the alpha or omega of the data, I am a facilitator. Because I have had conversations with the subjects of this essay as well as enlisted them in reading excerpts, in large part, the players are also the intended audience.

Next, though it is obvious this essay is centered on men, my existence as well as this work would not have been possible without the women in my life. Because a child's first teacher is its mother, I am eternally grateful to mine, Sandra Woods, who joined the ancestors in 2014. She was the perfect nurturer to her first child. Mom's compassion, cooking, creativity, unique sense of humor and eternal optimism have given me much to live up to.

My grandmothers on both sides are also worthy to be praised. My grandmother on my father's side, Mary Woods, cleaned homes for a living while raising nine children, including her youngest, my father Esmo. She kept a bowl of fruit on her kitchen table and always had a family story to tell whenever we visited. She passed not long after our family moved to Pontiac, Michigan in 1969. Then there was my grandmother on my mother's side, Lillian Dixon, whom I mentioned in Chapter Four whom I was living with while going to college. She lived to be nearly 101, before also peacefully joining the ancestors in 2010.

Moreover, my sister Christina was a sounding board for this work as we sometimes debated many of the ideas. In addition to family, I would like to extend a heartfelt thanks to the wives of the men who were a part of the study. You can't have a father of five boys (some are men), Sam Mims, without there being a mother, his wife, Michelle. In fact, "Man Code 2:4 I'm going to respect you and you are going to respect me" is her baby. Beside every great man is a great woman. Mark Johnson's wife, Sonya, and a former teaching colleague as well, gave me some feedback on a section of this work.

Of course, I would be remiss if I didn't recognize my deceased wife Krystal who transitioned in 1998 while pursuing her medical degree. At that time, I was only attempting to reciprocate the assistance she provided when I received my doctorate in 1996.

I must commend Ms. Terri Swift, math and science educator extraordinaire, for standing with me as we embraced our villainization for holding the school leadership team, including a gentleman discussed in 3:4, accountable. We were armed with the truth and dangerous because we weren't shy about sharing it with others. I can joke about it now, but it seemed as if she and I "stayed in trouble."

Because teaching, even at the high school level, is a female-dominated occupation, I would not have enjoyed a career that spanned four decades without the support and guidance of my dynamic and resourceful female counterparts. These women also were a proving ground for many of my theories, because I was able to run ideas by them and also learn from their perspectives as wives, mothers, and girlfriends.

We definitely had each other's back. When some of the girls would come crying to me about my female peers, I would laugh and remind the young ladies that they should one day hope to emulate the level of professionalism of these women as well as their character. On a personal note, I could speak to the girls about how my co-workers' brilliance as educators was only exceeded by their success as partners and parents. I spoke from seeing it myself.

Many times, we had the same students, so they would help me communicate to the boys several of the main principles: sit up straight, open your mouth when speaking, stop going back and forth with the girls in the class, and make eye contact when communicating, especially with adults. Although some of the traits could work well with the girls too, as a man, I had to drive these points home, because I wanted the boys to mature and take on a leadership role in the community. It definitely takes a village.

The man principles were particularly effective in promoting my program's behavioral goals. It was typical for me to be talking to female heads of houses during parent conferences. I got buy-in from the vast majority when I expressed my desire for the boys to learn how to be productive, independent contributors to society, in addition to being a "good student." My real aim was for the girls to become women, and the boys to become **men**.

To that end, a young colleague of mine, Mr. Dennis Veal, an assistant principal, who was a freshman social studies teacher at the time, invited me to be a guest presenter for his ninth grade boys' club. I gave them the Man Matrix, a binary chart with a matching quiz which drew distinctions between the conduct of boys and men. Perhaps because I had frequently engaged these young men at our small high school on an informal basis anyway, most of them got nearly all the items correct! I have included a copy of this simple quiz after the Epilogue for your perusal.

Now I would like to share two choices I grappled with in the creation of this document. First, is the use of autobiography. As I was writing, I was constantly questioning the insertion of personal examples into the analysis. After careful consideration, I decided there was nothing wrong with my fingerprints being all over the evidence along with the other men portrayed here. I lost my objection over this because one should write about what **they know**. Even "objective" accounts contain a frame of reference, a point of view, if you will, and the selection, placement, and prominence of items always involves subjectivity.

Second, even though a plethora of professions were represented in the Man Code, I also struggled with the dominance of educational vignettes. Once again, my professional war stories won out because, for one, they were familiar accounts. A second and more important reason why I stopped fighting the use of the schoolhouse in my essay is because the core mission of the field of education is teaching and learning. What better context to draw from? In addition, despite the fact many of the lessons involved kids, they weren't the only ones getting "schooled."

I became not just a better teacher but a better man because of what I inferred from my colleagues as well as **the children**. As my career progressed, I tried to practice Wooden's philosophy that the "players had brains too," and attempted to involve the students as much as possible in their own training and development. On that note, the "cautionary tales" presented were a gross misrepresentation of a typical day at work. I used these non-fictional samples to connect to the themes of each chapter. No students were ultimately harmed in the production of the story. Those whom got some "act right" deserved it. It was not uncommon for children to later be grateful for the structure we provided, even if some of it tended to be "hands-on." One reason the kids were fortunate we didn't ignore inappropriate behavior is because, as I would always remind them, "In the streets, they don't write referrals."

The average day in the academy, like anywhere else, was fairly mundane. What was not included was nearly each day was filled with learning, laughter, and love. The good experiences **far**, and I do mean **far** outweighed the bad! The long career I enjoyed in the Detroit Public Schools Community District was easily one of the most gratifying experiences of my life. The district took a chance on me as a substitute teacher in 1984, and despite being laid off and brought back a few times, I never looked back until my retirement in 2018. A highlight of my career was a classroom visit by the superintendent, Dr. Nikolai Vitti, during my final year of teaching. I owe a great debt to the district, the students, staff and parents, and the city of Detroit as a whole for receiving me as they did!

The term educare is latin for "to bring out." The scenes contained in the Man Code all had morals attached to them, what we were trying to "bring out" was the truth. The Codes may not pass judgment, but **life does**. Whenever a subject of the critique met with regrettable circumstances, it wasn't to be patronizing. In fact, the parables make it clear that it's easy to make mistakes. But that does not make them right, we must learn from them and move on. When we continue to make the same miscues, the piper must be paid.

Raise your hand if you have felt tempted to do the following: 1) Take your anger out on a loved one 2) Mouth off in public 3) Blow up on a supervisor at work 4) Walk off the job 5) Hang out somewhere that you knew was dangerous but exciting. If your hand went up for any or even all five, you passed the test—YOU'RE HUMAN!!

As you have read, 1-5 were actual predicaments protagonists faced in this analysis. But most of us have made it this far because we have **resisted the temptation to do them**. Just because you can do something, doesn't make it a good idea.

Last but not least, I would like to thank my personal Fab Five Man Circle of elders: My father, Mr. Esmo Woods, Attorney Mr. Elbert Hatchett, my Uncles Booker Woods (father's side) and William Redmond (mother's side), and Grandfather Samuel Dixon, the latter three, may they rest in peace. To all the ancestors and mancestors from time immemorial, may the dawning of a new day reach another generation because of the blessings bestowed on it by the Codes!

Peace!

# MATCHING MAN QUIZ

## *The Man Code Forum/Dr. Woods*

**Directions: Match the misguided behavior on the left with how someone operating on the Man Code would respond on the right:**

Man Code definition: A code of behavior followed by conscious adult males.

| MISGUIDED BOY | MAN CODE |
|---|---|
| 1. Will talk a good game, but can't back it up | A. Wants to improve and is receptive to guidance, instruction, correction and discipline (Man training), especially from those providing Man concepts |
| 2. Argues or goes into a shell when asked a question he doesn't want to answer, talks out of turn | B. Faces challenges head on, welcomes constructive criticism |

3. Has head down, not aware of immediate environment (makes himself a mark)

C. Makes eye contact, especially when addressing an elder

4. Only listens to the wrong crowd, insubordinate, unruly, wild, and incorrigible

D. Protects, provides, and proclaims, capable of paying bills (legally), can look out for self/ others, knows people don't owe him anything, so he appreciates what others do for him

5. Runs out of the room or runs away when challenged

E. Knows when to be quiet, speaks when necessary and when spoken to

6. Can only make bills, takes others assistance for granted, and always expects people to take care of him

F. Head on a swivel at all times (on point because he knows security is Manlaw)

7. Scared to look a man in the eyes

G. Says what he means, and means what he says

## Five things real men never say:

1. "I'm irritated" (a man's job is to deal with irritation)

2. "They made me do it" (real men control their own destinies)

3. "I'm going to tell _____ on you" (a man can solve his own problems)

4. "I'm about to go off" (men must learn to control their emotions, and rarely advertise their moves to the enemy)

5. "Don't talk to me" (now you sound as if you are in preschool)

## Key for Man Quiz

1. G

2. E

3. F

4. A

5. B

6. D

7. C

# REFERENCES AND RECOMMENDED READING

Album, Mitch. *The Fab Five.* New York: Warner Books, 1993.

Aromondo, A., & Evans, A. (Producers), & Podhertz, J. (Director). (2017). *Celtics/Lakers: The Best of Enemies.* [Video file]. Retrieved from https: en.wikipedia.org/wiki/Celtics/Lakers_Best_of_Enemies

Bernstein, R., & Edelman, E., & Greenberg, R., & Lavine, J., & Rohatgi, R. (Producers), & Edelman, E. (Director). (2010). *Magic & Bird: A Courtship of Rivals* [Video file]. Retrieved from https: en.wikipedia.org/Magic_%26_Bird:_A_Courtship_of_Rivals

Brennan, N., & Claybrooks, M., & Hernandez, T., & Skidmore, J., & Storer, C. (Producers), & Brennan, N. (Director). (2018). *Chris Rock: Tamborine.* [Netflix Special]. Retrieved from https: en.wikipedia.org/wiki/Chris_Rock:_Tamborine

Christoper, Matt. *On the Court With...Dwight Howard.* New York: Little Brown Books for Young Readers, 2002.

Cervantes, Miguel. *El cerco de Numancia.* Madrid: Biblioteca Nacional de Espana, 1585.

Davis, Miles, and Trope, Quincy. *Miles: The Autobiography of Miles Davis with Quincy Trope.* New York: Simon and Schuster, 1989.

Donner, L., & Donner, R., & Halsted, D., & Stone, O., & Townsend, C. (Producers), & Stone, O. (Director). (1999). *Any Given Sunday.* [Motion Picture]. United States: Warner Brothers.

Gretky, Wayne, and Day, Kristie M. *Stories of the Game.* New York: G.P. Putnam's Sons, 2016.

Griffin, Archie, and Diles, Dave. *Archie: The Archie Griffin Story.* New York: Knopf Doubleday Publishing, 1977.

Guber, P., & Portnoy, E., & Tollin, M., (Producers), & Hehir, J. (Director). (2020). *The Last Dance: Episode 10.* [Video file]. Retrieved from https: en.wikipedia.org/wiki/The_Last_Dance_(miniseries)

Harcourt, Alexander H., Stewart, Kelly J. *Gorilla Society: Conflict, Compromise, and Cooperation Between the Sexes.* University of Chicago Press, 2008.

Henry, S. (Producer & Director). (2001). *ESPN SportsCentury: Isiah Thomas* [Video file]. Retrieved from https: imdb.com/title/tt05682791

"Allen Iverson." *Georgetown Basketball History.* December 3, 2010. Archived from the original on February 14, 2012. Retrieved on October 31, 2020.

Jackson, Phil, and Delehanty, Hugh. *Eleven Rings.* New York: Penguin Books, 2013.

Kipling, Rudyard. *The Jungle Book.* New York: Macmillan, 1894.

Labi, Nadya. *"THE HIT MAN'S TALE: How an honors student became a hired killer."* New Yorker. October 15, 2012 Issue. Retrieved from https: newyorker.com/magazine/2012/'10/'15/the-hit-mans-tale/

Miller, Percy. *Guaranteed Success: When You Never Give Up.* New York: Kensington Publishing, 2007.

Myers, Walter Dean. *The Greatest: The Life of Muhammad Ali.* New York: Scholastic, 2001.

Neuhaus, A. (Producer), & Mitchell, F. (Director). (2019). *Saturdays in the South: A History of SEC Football: Star Power (Episode Five).* [Video file]. Retrieved from https: imdb.com/title/tt11092558/

Nicklaus, Jack, and Bowden, Ken. *Jack Nicklaus: My Story.* New York: Simon and Schuster, 1984.

Obama, Michelle. *Becoming.* New York: Penguin Publishing, 2018.

Perrow, Charles. *Complex Organizations: A Critical Essay (Third Edition).* New York: McGraw Hill, 1986.

Sanders, Barry, and Heffron, Jack. *Barry Sanders Now You See Him...:In His Own Words.* Evanston, IL: Emmis, 2005.

Taubman, A. Alfred. *A. Alfred Taubman Papers: 1942-2014 (Biography)*. Bentley Historical Library, University of Michigan. Retrieved from https: quod.lib.umich.edu/b/bhlead/umich-bhl-2011097?view=text/

Turner, J. (2020, August, 31). *"'Never run when you are right' Whistleblower of the week: Frank Serpico."* Retrieved from https: whistleblowersblog.org/2020/08/articles/whistleblower-of-the-week/whistleblower-of-the-week-frank-serpico-never-run-when-you-are-right/

Tyson, Mike. *Undisputed Truth*. New York: HarperCollins, 2013.

Tzu, Sun, and Cleary, Thomas (Translation). *The Art of War*. Boston & London: Shambala, 1991.

Wooden, John, and Jamison, Steve. *My Personal Best: Life Lessons from an All-American Journey*. New York: McGraw Hill Professional, 2004.

Wooden, John, and Jamison, Steve. *Wooden: A Lifetime of Observations and Reflections On and Off the Court*. New York: McGraw Hill, 1997.

Zbynek, Zaba. *Le Maximes de Ptahhotep*. Prague: Academie Tchecoslovaque des Sciences, 1956.